As one of the world's longest established and best-known travel brands, Thomas Cook are the experts in travel.

For more than 135 years our guidebooks have unlocked the secrets of destinations around the world, sharing with travellers a wealth of experience and a passion for travel.

Rely on Thomas Cook as your travelling companion on your next trip and benefit from our unique heritage.

Thomas Cook **traveller** guides

MALTA & GOZO
Susie Boulton

Your travelling companion since 1873

Written by Susie Boulton, updated by David Browne

Published by Thomas Cook Publishing
A division of Thomas Cook Tour Operations Limited
Company registration no. 3772199 England
The Thomas Cook Business Park, Unit 9, Coningsby Road,
Peterborough PE3 8SB, United Kingdom
Email: books@thomascook.com, Tel: + 44 (0) 1733 416477
www.thomascookpublishing.com

Produced by Cambridge Publishing Management Limited
Burr Elm Court, Main Street, Caldecote CB23 7NU
www.cambridgepm.co.uk

ISBN: 978-1-84848-367-5

© 2002, 2005, 2007, 2009 Thomas Cook Publishing
This fifth edition © 2011
Text © Thomas Cook Publishing
Maps © Thomas Cook Publishing/PCGraphics (UK) Limited

Series Editor: Karen Beaulah
Production/DTP: Steven Collins

Printed and bound in Spain by GraphyCems

Cover photography © Reinhard Schmid/SIME-4Corners Images

Contents

Introduction

'Malta – that tiny rock of history and romance.'
WINSTON CHURCHILL
The Second World War, 1948

Malta and Gozo draw over a million visitors a year. The islands are a year-round place to visit – and not only for the abundant sunshine and sea. They have a rich cultural heritage with prehistoric temples, ornate palaces and churches betraying a Christian tradition that the Maltese trace back to the shipwreck of St Paul the Apostle.

Malta is popular with British holidaymakers because it is barely three hours' flying time from London, there is plenty of relatively cheap accommodation and most residents are fluent in English – a legacy of about 150 years of British rule. Entry into the European Union and adoption of the euro has also widened Malta's appeal, as has a constant flow of English language students.

Malta and Gozo have also grown as playgrounds for the rich and famous, with prestige spa hotel resorts and yachting marinas providing plenty of attractions for visitors seeking luxury breaks.

THOMAS COOK'S MALTA

The opening of the Suez Canal in 1869 inspired Thomas Cook and his son to open an office in Cairo. Malta was a steamer stop en route to Egypt and 21 years later a Thomas Cook office was established here. Affluent British visitors began coming in the spring and autumn in search of the sun. The 20th century saw the arrival of summer holidaymakers, and in the years following World War II, Malta started to develop its seaside resorts.

The mild winter months and springtime are wonderful for walking and birdwatching. Cultural events such as concerts, sailing and powerboat racing, religious celebrations and arts festivals are a big draw.

The clear waters containing sunken ships and aircraft have made the islands a prime destination for diving. The Valletta Waterfront is a regular stop for Mediterranean cruise liners, and the opening of air routes to low-cost carriers has made Malta more accessible for short breaks from Britain and Europe.

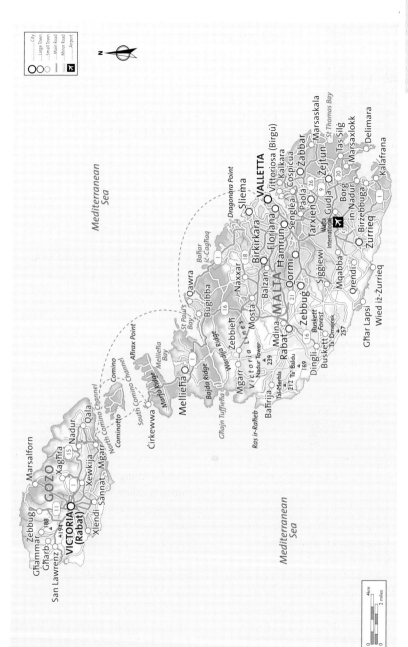

The land

The Maltese islands lie in the centre of the Mediterranean, 93km (58 miles) south of Sicily and 300km (186 miles) north of Libya. The archipelago is made up of the islands of Malta, Gozo and Comino, plus the tiny uninhabited islets of Cominotto in the north and Filfla, off the southern coast. Together, the islands make up a mere 316sq km (122sq miles). Malta, the largest of them, is only 27km (17 miles) at its longest point from northwest to southeast, and 14.5km (9 miles) at its widest point, from west to east.

Climate

Malta's climate is typical of the Mediterranean, with long hot summers, warm and sporadically wet autumns, and cool but unpredictable winters. Malta has an annual average of eight hours of sunshine a day.

Population

With a population of around 410,000, Malta is the most densely populated country in Europe. The vast majority of people live in Valletta and the surrounding area. Gozo has a population of approximately 31,000.

Landscape

The island of Malta consists of a gently undulating limestone plateau. There are no mountains, rivers or lakes, and the land looks rocky and barren, particularly in summer. This arid appearance is emphasised by the scores of drystone walls.

To ease the water shortage on the island, five reverse-osmosis plants have been set up on the coast to convert seawater to fresh water, and these plants now produce half of the water consumed in Malta.

The Maltese woodlands were hacked down centuries ago, and today the only trees you will see are the carob, pine, citrus, ficus and tamarisk that have been planted in public parks, along avenues and around town piazzas. On both Malta and Gozo the slopes are cultivated for vegetables and vines.

For centuries the country's abundant limestone has been put to use for construction – from prehistoric megaliths to modern-day houses. Newly quarried stone soon mellows with exposure to the sun and blends with the colour of the surroundings. The most widely used limestone today is the soft globigerina.

Because of its greater quantity of water-retaining blue clay subsoil, Gozo is a greener island than Malta. The lie of the land is different, with villages built on flat-topped hills, leaving the slopes for cultivation.

The coastline

The coastline of Malta and Gozo is predominantly rocky, with only a very occasional sandy bay. Most of the beaches are rocky. Malta's coastline is heavily indented. The eastern side of the island is broken up by large bays which make ideal natural harbours. To the south, spectacular cliffs drop 250m (820ft) to the sea. Gozo's coastal scenery is at its most spectacular around the cliffs of Dwejra.

The economy

Tourism is Malta's prime industry, accounting for around a third of the country's gross national product. The number of annual visitors is 1.2 million, which is almost three times the population of the islands.

The country has seen a shift away from traditional labour-intensive manufacturing services towards banking services and information technology. Film production is a growing industry, with a number of international blockbusters shot here in recent years, such as *Troy*, *Alexander* and scenes in *The Da Vinci Code*.

Despite the thin, dry soil, agriculture is a mainstay of the economy. The main vegetables are potatoes and onions. Grapes, the largest fruit crop, produce wine for local consumption and export.

Clusters of dense urban settlements dot the fertile agricultural land

The people

Maltese people are by nature friendly and hospitable, although noticeably less ebullient than their Italian neighbours. The Maltese are a proud and resilient nation with a history of foreign domination down the centuries. They respect family values and are devoted to children. Observance of age-old religious traditions is important to Maltese families and a festa (village street party) to honour a saint is not put on just to entertain tourists.

Gozitans are slightly different from the Maltese and an amicable rivalry exists between the two islands. Gozitans, of necessity, have always been hard-working and thrifty, but are accused by the Maltese of being penny-pinching and go-getting. If this is true, it is certainly not apparent to the casual visitor. Gozitans seem every bit as friendly and hospitable as the Maltese.

Dress

The attitude towards dress is not as liberal as it is in some European countries. Topless bathing or sunbathing is against the law, and may well offend the locals. In secluded spots, however, such as a beach in Ġnejna Bay, nudism is tolerated. Sauntering around streets or hotels in skimpy clothes or swimwear is also frowned upon. As in most Catholic countries, the wearing of miniskirts, shorts or sleeveless garments in churches is likely to cause offence. Some of the most frequently visited churches provide shawls and skirts to cover offending parts – but nothing for men, who are best advised to wear long trousers and short-sleeved shirts for church visiting. In most restaurants and hotels, dress is smart but casual. Some of the best restaurants are in four- or five-star hotels where men may need to wear a jacket.

Language

Malta has two official languages – English and Maltese. Maltese is a fascinating language, reflecting a host of different influences. Its roots are Arabic; later, under the rule of various European powers, it absorbed a smattering of Italian (mainly Sicilian), Spanish, French and English.

The official language of the Order of St John was Italian. Since Maltese had no written form (and at that stage was a very basic language), literate Maltese people tended to speak Italian too. When the British arrived they rather expected, in true imperial fashion, that local people would simply drop Italian and pick up English overnight. In fact, it was not until 1921 that English became the official administrative language of the island.

Maltese did not have a standardised alphabet until 1924. It is written in modified Roman characters, which seems incongruous for a language that sounds so Arabic, and one in which God is called Allah. Today, you can almost draw a dividing line between the real Maltese villages, where Maltese is very much the first language, and the more sophisticated areas (such as Sliema), where English is considered the superior language and learnt from the cradle. Between these two extremes are the many Maltese inhabitants who speak half and half.

For an English-speaking visitor to Malta there is absolutely no need to try to master the Maltese language. All signs and notices are bilingual, and the vast majority of locals speak English, many of them fluently, albeit with a characteristic sing-song intonation. The Maltese are good linguists, and many speak fluent Italian and French as well. Italian remains particularly popular because the Maltese have a choice of a dozen or so Italian TV channels, so children pick up the language quite easily.

The people

Fishing retains an important place in the lives of these island people

Enjoying the pleasures of conversation in the open air

The Maltese lifestyle

In keeping with Mediterranean customs, most Maltese enjoy a siesta on summer afternoons. This lasts for two or three hours after lunch, during which time the majority of shops are closed. As a tourist you are best advised to follow suit and emerge again in the early hours of the evening, when the temperature is more pleasant, and the Maltese go out for an evening stroll, called the *passiġġata.*

Patriotism

With good reason the Maltese are passionately proud of their culture and history. On the other hand, living on a group of small islands has inevitably led to a certain insularity. While many Maltese, and particularly those who have travelled, are very cosmopolitan, others see their islands as the cultural centre of the world. This is despite the conspicuous influence of foreign cultures, and the strong links that the locals have always maintained with Maltese emigrants.

Women

Until relatively recently Maltese society was very male-dominated, most wives readily accepting their place in the home where they had no legal authority over their property, or even over their children. However, legislation has now given women equal rights, and the number of working mothers is on the increase. As women are gradually becoming more independent and confident, the men are slowly losing their traditional status as head of the household.

Female visitors to Malta need not feel threatened by local males. The islands are comparatively safe, and women are unlikely to encounter anything more troublesome than the roving Mediterranean eye.

Statue of St Nicholas, patron saint of the village of Siġġiewi

History

Around 5000 BC	Neolithic farmers arrive.
5000– 4000 BC	Neolithic period. Skorba temples built.
4000– 3000 BC	Temple period. Age of Tarxien and Ġgantija temples and Ħal Saflieni Hypogeum.
2500– 700 BC	Bronze and Iron Ages. Period of fortified villages and 'cart tracks'.
700–550 BC	Phoenicians colonise the islands.
550–218 BC	Period of Carthaginian rule.
218 BC	Romans annex Malta in their strategy to win the Second Punic War.
AD 60	St Paul is shipwrecked on Malta, and brings Christianity to the island.
5th century	Roman power diminishes; Vandal raids.
6th century	The Byzantine Empire gains control.
870	The Arabs conquer Malta.
1090	Roger the Norman, ruler of Sicily and parts of southern Italy, takes Malta from the Arabs.
1194	Malta (with Sicily) becomes part of the German Hohenstaufen Empire.
1266	Charles of Anjou takes over the kingdom of Sicily, of which Malta is a part.
1282	Riots against French rule in Sicily. King Pedro I of Aragon defeats Charles of Anjou; Sicily and Malta come under the kingdom of Aragon.
1429	Malta sacked by Muslims.
Mid-15th century	Emergence of a *università*, or local governing body, under Aragonese tutelage.
Early 16th century	Having declined both economically and culturally, Malta is now reduced to little more than a geographic entity with only 20,000 inhabitants.

1530	Emperor Charles V of Spain grants the Maltese islands to the Knights of the Order of St John of Jerusalem. The Knights occupy the islands, making Birgù (modern Vittoriosa) their headquarters.
1565	The Great Siege of Malta.
1566	The city of Valletta is founded.
1571	The Maltese capital is formally moved from Birgù to Valletta. A Christian fleet, assisted by the Knights, inflicts defeat on the Ottomans at Lepanto.
1676	Plague causes 8,569 deaths.
1693	Earthquake wrecks most of Mdina.
1735	Sicilian ports are closed to Maltese ships after Grand Master de Vilhena resists Charles VIII's attempt to influence Maltese affairs.
Late 18th century	The Order becomes demilitarised and corrupted by wealth.

1792	The French National Assembly confiscates the Order's lands in France.
1798	Napoleon takes Malta and plunders the islands. The Order of St John is made to leave the island. The Maltese rise up against the French; helped by the British, they besiege the main French garrison.
1800	The French capitulate and the British occupy the island.

Statue of the Madonna in Mdina

An early map of Valletta

1802	The Treaty of Amiens stipulates that Malta should be returned to the Knights, but a powerful group of Maltese declares allegiance to Britain.	
1813	Sir Thomas Maitland is appointed first British Governor of Malta.	
1814	The Treaty of Paris formally recognises Malta as a British Crown Colony.	
1869	The opening of the Suez Canal makes Malta an important port on the British route to India.	
1914–18	World War I. Malta becomes 'the Nurse of the	

Mediterranean', providing 25,000 beds for the wounded.

1919 Four Maltese men, part of a riot over the price of bread, are shot by British troops.

1921 Malta is granted self-government 'in matters of local concern'.

1940 Italy enters World War II.

1942 The Second Great Siege. Over 6,000 tonnes of bombs are dropped on Malta in April alone. The George Cross is awarded to the Maltese people for their bravery during the air raids. In August the German and Italian air forces suffer heavy losses over Malta, and in October they concede defeat. The UK government gives £30 million for the reconstruction of the island.

1962 The State of Malta formally comes into being.

1964 Malta is granted full independence within the British Commonwealth.

1974 Malta is declared a republic.

1979 British forces leave.

1990 Malta applies for full membership of the European Community.

1996 The Nationalists are ousted by the Labour Party in elections.

1998 Nationalist victory puts the island back on course to join the European Union.

2004 On 1 May the Republic of Malta joins the European Union.

2008 The euro replaces the Maltese lira. The ruling National Party scores a narrow win over Labour in the general election.

2009 After years of growth, Malta experiences a severe dip in tourist numbers as a result of the global economic crisis.

2010 Politicians openly debate changing the law to allow divorce in Malta. Bus drivers protest at government plans to nationalise public transport and introduce modern buses.

Statue of four Maltese who were shot in the riots of 7 June 1919

The Great Siege

The Great Siege of Malta was one of the most remarkable military showdowns between Muslim and Christian, between the might of the Crescent and the forces of the Cross. In 1565 the Knights of St John, with some 9,000 men, defended the tiny island against a Turkish force of 40,000 men and 180 ships.

Well before the siege began it was common knowledge that Suleiman the Magnificent, the Sultan of Turkey, was planning to annihilate those 'sons of dogs'.

Christendom was not united, and for most of the four-month siege, the Knights were left to go it alone.

A scene from 'The Great Siege of Malta' walk-through experience in Valletta

They were, however, renowned for their physical courage and, as the historian Edward Gibbon sardonically put it, they 'neglected to live, but were prepared to die, in the service of Christ'.

The Turkish commander, Piali Pasha, began the siege with an attack on Fort St Elmo. The defenders fought to the death, pouring down cauldrons of pitch and hoops of fire. The Turks eventually took the fort, but they lost 8,000 men to 1,500 Christians. The handful of surviving Knights were butchered, nailed to crosses and floated out of the Grand Harbour. Not to be outdone in barbarity, Grand Master La Valette ordered the severed heads of Turkish prisoners to be cannon-fired into the enemy camp.

The Turks then turned their attention to Birgù, mercilessly firing a barrage at the buildings until they breached the fortress walls. Even so, their casualties were huge: on a single day they lost some 2,500 men. On 6 September the Viceroy of Sicily finally sent modest reinforcements to support the Knights.

The crafty La Valette released a Turkish prisoner, having tricked him into believing that the relief force was enormous. When this news was conveyed to the Muslims, it proved to be the last straw. Demoralised by fever and dysentery, the Turks evacuated the island of Malta on 8 September and sailed back to Constantinople, entering the city under cover of darkness out of shame.

The Christian world had watched with bated breath. Now, even the Protestant English Queen Elizabeth I gave orders for thanksgiving prayers to be said.

See p155 for the Great Siege Events Museum.

Malta being defended by the Knights of St John during the Great Siege

Politics

Maltese people are serious and enthusiastic about politics, as shown by turnouts of more than 90 per cent at elections. Debates and political meetings are always lively events and the rivalry is intense between the two main parties, the Nationalists (Christian Democrats) and the Labour Party (Social Democrats). Members of Parliament are elected by a system of proportional representation. Domestic issues dominate but Malta is seeking a big role in EU and Mediterranean regional affairs.

Malta was a British colony from 1814 and gained independence in September 1964. Malta is now a parliamentary republic within the Commonwealth. The president is the constitutional head of state but executive powers are held by the House of Representatives and the government is led by the prime minister. There are 69 members of the single-chamber parliament, who sit in the Grand Master's Palace in Valletta. Support for the two main parties is evenly divided. In the elections in 2008 the Nationalists won by a narrow margin over the Labour Party. In 2009 George Abela, a Labour politician, became the first president to come from an opposition party.

In the 1970s and 1980s Maltese politics was dominated by the charismatic Labour leader Dom Mintoff, who forged links with Russia, China and Libya. Elections in 1987 brought the Nationalists to power and ushered in a greater emphasis on partnership with Europe.

Malta joined the European Union in 2004. Membership of the EU brought rewards and Malta has benefited from economic growth not only in tourism but also in financial services, information technology and pharmaceuticals.

The downside is that the resulting influx of illegal migrants, especially from north Africa, has put great strain on Malta's resources and the government is constantly lobbying Brussels for aid as this is seen as an EU border problem. There are also regular ministerial meetings with Libya to address this issue and shared concerns about oil exploration and fishing in the Mediterranean region.

In 2008 Malta adopted the euro as its currency. Fears that the changeover would cause price increases have never gone away and you will still see prices in markets and on till receipts expressed in Maltese liras alongside the official euro price.

Malta has been suffering from the effects of the global recession, and the tourism industry in particular took a hit with a drop in visitor numbers in 2009 and 2010 after many years of sustained growth. Malta avoided the worst of the economic crisis because its banks operate mainly in local business and had not got entangled in complex foreign debt deals.

The prime minister's office is located in the Auberge de Castille et Léon in Valletta

Culture

Malta's strategic setting at the crossroads of the Mediterranean shipping lanes has always played a crucial role in the islands' history. Over the centuries the great Mediterranean powers have fought to dominate the islands, each leaving its legacy. The Arabs introduced citrus trees and flat-topped houses, and laid the foundations for the Maltese language, and the Aragonese, from central Spain, left their mark on the medieval architecture of Malta's historic town centres.

Architecture

Under the 268-year rule of the Knights of St John, Malta blossomed into a major cultural centre. The buildings they put up touched on almost every sphere of human activity, from water distribution to heavy fortifications. By the time the British arrived at the start of the 19th century, Malta was at the forefront of European culture in terms of its architecture. In turn, the British developed the island for both military and commercial purposes.

The words which come most readily to mind in characterising Maltese architecture are religion, defence and limestone. Neolithic people left their mark in the mighty temples to their gods, while the long, continuous Christian tradition has given rise to huge and ever-more splendid edifices to the glory of God. The island's defences are equally eloquent, as can be seen in the siting of Arab Mdina, or the fortifications of Aragonese Birgù (now Vittoriosa), or in the obsessive and interminable military building of the Knights. Malta is above all a fortress, and the mighty defensive system, shoring up Valletta, Floriana and the Three Cities, is one of the greatest exhibitions of pre-modern Christian military architecture to be seen anywhere in the world.

The great architectural tool of all these builders was, and remains, the abundant honey-coloured globigerina limestone, easily cut and pleasingly mellow to the eye.

The church and community

Malta's long Christian tradition dates from AD 60 when St Paul was shipwrecked on the island. In spite of Islamic and other cultural influences, Catholicism has always been a dominant force in Maltese life, influencing social, political and even economic issues. Around 98 per cent of the population are Catholic and 52.6 per cent attend Mass weekly – one of the highest rates in Europe.

The village *festa*, celebrating the local patron saint, plays an essential role in cementing community spirit, and there is intense rivalry among the different parishes which compete to mount the most spectacular parades and firework displays.

Further evidence of religious conviction is the abundance of street-corner shrines, from the finely carved to the crude and garishly coloured. Even some of the old-fashioned buses have a little shrine inside, and a conspicuous 'Jesus loves me' sticker beneath.

The churches of Malta and Gozo are primarily Baroque in style. The great architect of the 16th century, Gerolamo Cassar, designed St John's Co-Cathedral in addition to the Knights' *auberges*, the fortifications and several other churches in Valletta.

The 17th century saw the rise of another great Maltese architect, Lorenzo Gafà, whose work is best seen in the parish churches and cathedrals of Mdina and Gozo. Splendid domes are a hallmark of Maltese churches, their huge dimensions dwarfing the surrounding village houses.

The grandiose interiors have gilded arcades and ceilings, intricately ornate altars and canopies. Walls and vaults are covered in paintings and frescoes, the principal exponent being the Italian master Mattia Preti, who decorated St John's Co-Cathedral and numerous other churches throughout Malta with his Baroque art.

Arts and crafts

Malta's once-flagging arts and crafts industry has been given a big boost by tourism. Craft villages on both Malta and Gozo have been set up to demonstrate (and sell) all the traditional handicrafts. Although outside these villages the artisan is a dying breed, you can still occasionally glimpse a fisherman weaving cane into fish traps, a farmer's wife making baskets for eggs, or, in Gozo, an old woman skilfully making lace in the streets.

Floats and parades are an essential part of Maltese culture

Religion

The vast majority of Maltese are devout Catholics and the clergy are respected figures locally and nationally. The Catholic faith is enshrined in the Constitution as the state religion and the Church is still the focal point of community life. Questions about moral issues, such as a law to permit divorce, are debated passionately and religious education has a key role in schools.

Everywhere you look in Malta you will see a church, partly because there are so many but also because they are so large. The parish church is always the biggest building in a village, dwarfing the houses.

The Maltese are proud of their religious heritage, which they trace back to biblical times and the shipwreck of St Paul, recorded in the New Testament. The period of rule by the Knights of St John of Jerusalem has also left a religious legacy, particularly in church architecture.

The Constitution establishes the Catholic faith as the official religion of Malta but also guarantees freedom of worship for all other religions. There is a mosque on Corradino Hill in Paola and for many years a ground-floor flat in St Ursula Street in Valletta served as Malta's only synagogue – funds are being raised to replace it. St Paul's Pro-Cathedral in Valletta is the main Anglican church in Malta.

Saints' days and other major Christian feasts are celebrated vigorously in Malta, sometimes for several days, with street parties, music, parades and fireworks. Good Friday is a particularly sombre time with solemn processions, but Easter Day is a blaze of joy, music and family get-togethers.

There is no doubt that the Maltese are devout and church attendance is above average for Europe. But the strains of modern secularism are showing and fewer young people are quite as rigorous in their attendance – many will tell you that they go to church only to please their mothers.

Parish priest leading a church procession

Hooded *penitentes* carry life-size statues through the streets before Easter

Festivals

Festivals are an important part of Maltese cultural life. Many have their roots in religious traditions, such as celebrating the feast day of a village patron saint or observing the major feasts of the Christian calendar such as Easter. The festivities can last several days and include parades, brass bands and fireworks. Other festivals celebrate national achievements, the arts, music and wine, and joining in a festival can be a highlight of a visit to Malta.

Throughout the summer, villages and towns celebrate the feast days of their parish patron saints. A complete list of village *festas* is available from the Archdiocese of Malta:
http://maltadiocese.org

Feast of St Paul's Shipwreck
10 February, Valletta
The centrepiece of this festival is a colourful parade from the Church of St Paul's Shipwreck. A carved wooden statue of the saint is accompanied by brass bands, with buildings festooned with banners and confetti thrown from balconies.

Carnival
Five days leading up to Ash Wednesday
The main activities are around Valletta, with street parties, games, dance competitions and parades of dancers in exotic costumes. In Nadur the festivities are much stranger with people silently walking the village disguised in wigs and masks.

Easter
Processions on Good Friday are sombre with church bells replaced by the macabre sound of the *tuqtojta*, a rattle or clapper, as a sign of mourning. You can hear the strange sound best in Qormi and Żejtun. On Easter Sunday the atmosphere is much more joyful, especially in the Three Cities where statue-bearers run with the Risen Christ.

Għanafest (Folk Music Festival)
First weekend of June
An opportunity to experience the different styles of Maltese folk song, known as *għana*. The festival is held in the Argotti Gardens, Floriana.

St Peter and St Paul
29 June
Traditionally known as *Imnarja*, the festival begins with displays of fruit, vegetables, honey and wine, and stalls are set up to sell *pastizzi* (traditional cheese-filled pastries), *mqaret* (dates in pastry) and *qubbajt* (nougat made with almonds).

The Malta Arts Festival

First three weeks in July

The highlight of the cultural calendar with classical music, dance, visual art and drama. The main events take place in open-air venues, including the waterfronts in Valletta and Vittoriosa and the ruins of the Old Opera House. *Tel: (056) 21245168. Email: info@maltaartsfestival.com*

Malta Jazz Festival

Third weekend of July

Past performers include Chick Corea and Herbie Hancock. The venue is the Ta'Liesse Wharf with the Grand Harbour as a stunning backdrop. *Tel: (056) 21232515. http://maltajazzfestival.org*

Delicata Wine Festival

August

Four evenings of wine tasting and good food, in the Upper Barracca Gardens, Valletta, and again in the village of Nadur on Gozo in early September. *Delicata. Tel: (356) 21825199. www.delicata.com*

Victory Day

8 September

A feast day celebrating two historic events: the end of the Great Siege in 1565, and the capitulation of the Italians in World War II. A colourful rowing regatta takes place in the Grand Harbour with teams from villages competing in races in distinctive coloured boats.

Independence Day

21 September

Public holiday to celebrate Malta's independence in 1964.

Notte Bianca (White Night)

Last Saturday in September

A night-time festival of the arts and culture in the streets of Valletta. Museums, art galleries and state palaces open their doors free of charge until the early hours. *Tel: (056) 21232515. Email: info@nottebiancamalta.com*

Festival Mediterranea

Mid-autumn

Music concerts, exhibitions, walks and visits to archaeological sites promote Gozo's rich heritage.

Christmas

December

Churches are decorated with drapes in gold and bright red and restaurants lay on their own entertainment. A tradition introduced under British rule is the Christmas pantomime at the Manoel Theatre in Valletta.

Festa night

Impressions

Malta is a tiny island and – unless you are staying on the far northern or western side – you will be within easy striking distance of the main centres, museums and historic sites. Even so, the small size of the island can be deceptive: distances may be short, but the volume of traffic – particularly through Valletta's seemingly endless conurbation, and between Sliema and Mellieħa – can severely hamper your journey.

Beaches

Maltese waters are among the bluest and cleanest in the Mediterranean. There are no dangerous tides or currents, but sandy beaches are scarce. The main ones are Mellieħa Bay in the north, and the glorious beaches of Għajn Tuffieħa and Golden Bay on the west coast. On Gozo the only beach is Ramla Bay, a long stretch of ochre-coloured sands.

Any sandy beach will be packed in season. Swimming and sunbathing otherwise take place at hotel pools or from the rocky shorelines. In some of the larger resorts, such as Sliema, artificial lidos provide good swimming, often from flattened rock ledges. The very best swimming is inevitably found away from the built-up areas and usually entails a scramble down the cliffside. One of the loveliest spots of all is the **Blue Lagoon** off Comino – as long as you get there before the excursion boats. The main beaches provide facilities such as cafés, sunbeds, parasols, showers and watersports. Amenities for scuba diving are excellent, and windsurfing and sailing are also popular.

Boat trips

Travelling by boat is one of the best ways of getting to know the island. A day in Gozo is worthwhile for the ferry trip alone. Organised tour options include a cruise around all the islands, or an underwater safari on a glass-bottom boat. Don't take a boat trip on a particularly windy day.

A leisurely way to explore Malta

Resorts

Malta's biggest tourist resort, Sliema, has many facilities and easy access to most parts of the island. Further north, round St Paul's Bay, tourist development has stifled the fishing village. Mellieħa and the resorts beyond it are quite remote, but have good swimming, and are handy for trips to Comino and Gozo.

At Golden Bay, on the west of the island, development is limited to one hotel and nearby Għajn Tuffieħa remains unspoilt. In the east, the fishing village of Marsaskala is becoming popular, but picturesque Marsaxlokk remains very much a fishing village. In the south, high cliffs prevent development. For a quiet time, opt for Gozo, which is still relatively free of the trappings of mass tourism. Quieter still is the tiny island of Comino, with just one hotel and only a few permanent residents.

Sightseeing

Malta's chequered history provides a wealth of prehistoric and historic monuments. State-owned sites and museums are managed by Heritage Malta, whose entrance charges vary. Over 65s pay half the adult price. Children aged 6–11 pay a quarter, under-5s go free. Privately run museums have their own admission fees; these can range from €1 per adult to €8.

The main cultural centres are Valletta, Mdina and Rabat. The capital, Valletta, has enough museums, churches, palaces and bastions to keep you occupied for several days. Medieval Mdina is tiny but has a wealth of culture; nearby are the churches and catacombs of Rabat. Gozo's cultural hub is Victoria, which has a fine citadel.

In summer sightsee early to avoid the midday heat. The most important archaeological sites and Heritage Malta-run museums are open daily, including Sunday, from 9am to 5pm. Day tickets are available to museums and archaeological sites in the same area; for example, the Domus Romana, St Paul's Catacombs and the national Natural History Museum in Mdina and Rabat.

Churches and historic sites are found all over these islands

The British in Malta

'One felt the splendour of the British Empire, let the world say what it likes.'
D H LAWRENCE, 1924

After 160 years on Malta, it is not surprising that the British left their mark. British occupation began in 1800. Brigadier General Thomas Graham and his forces helped the Maltese drive out an occupying garrison of French Napoleonic soldiers; the Royal Navy also blockaded the islands. Malta and Gozo became a part of the British Empire and were used as the Mediterranean headquarters for the Royal Navy fleet. Malta finally achieved independence in 1964.

For ten years, Queen Elizabeth II remained as Queen of Malta, but, on 13 December 1974, Malta became a republic within the Commonwealth, with the president as head of state.

Winston Churchill is remembered in several places in Malta

The British legacy is apparent not so much in permanent monuments as in the little features of everyday Maltese life: the Bedford buses, the red pillar boxes and telephone kiosks, the special curry served on Sundays at the Sports Club in Marsa.

Of course, the British left big things as well: a constitution, a new legal system, a fine dockyard complex, a chain of forts and, in addition, various monuments to British monarchs and worthies.

On the minus side, the British created the first urban sprawl (around Valletta), and even thought about knocking down the capital's ancient

A Bedford bus

fortifications to make way for new housing. It was also British servicemen who named the red-light area of Valletta 'The Gut' and made it a notorious institution.

The majority of Maltese still have a fondness for all things British – whether that means memories of the war, the football scene, roast beef or royalty. The queen's visit in May 1992, planned to coincide with the 50th anniversary of the award to Malta of the George Cross, reaffirmed the links – as did a visit in 2007 marking her 60th wedding anniversary.

Given all this – and the fact that almost everyone speaks some English (because the British taught them to) – it comes as no surprise to learn that over 4,000 (about 1 per cent) of Malta's residents are British, and that of the 1.2 million or so people who visit Malta every year, nearly 40 per cent come from the United Kingdom.

The legacy of British occupation is visible in many small details

Valletta

The Knights of St John were quick to realise the potential of the slopes of Mount Sceberras and the great sweep of the surrounding harbour. Shortly after the epic siege of 1565, Francesco Laparelli was sent to Malta to advise on the building of a new city. The first stone was laid on 28 May 1566, and the city was completed just five years later. Over the next 20 years, the various auberges, *the residences for the Knights, as well as the Grand Master's Palace and the great Co-Cathedral of St John were designed and built.*

Today, the capital Valletta is still Malta's richest repository of art, architecture, history and culture. It is also the main shopping and business centre. Sightseeing could occupy two or three days, but equally rewarding are the walks round the ramparts or through the streets, many of which are flanked by handsome balconied houses, while the backstreets drop steeply down to the harbour.

THE AUBERGES

The Order of St John was divided into eight *langues* (or nationalities), each one having its own *auberge*. Literally translated as an 'inn' or 'hostel', this was more akin to an Oxford or Cambridge college, with a chapel, dining hall and accommodation ranged around a courtyard. Of the original *auberges*, five have survived, and only one is open to the public. The exteriors alone, however, give you a good idea of the lifestyle enjoyed by the Knights.

The original eight *auberges* were first established in Birgù (now Vittoriosa). The Knights then moved to grander premises in Valletta when that city was built. By this time there were only seven *auberges*, Henry VIII having suppressed the English *langue* after his conjugal quarrel with the Pope.

All the *auberges* were built by the Maltese architect Gerolamo Cassar between 1571 and 1590, although they were largely rebuilt during the 18th

THE MALTESE CROSS

The eight-pointed cross, known as the Maltese Cross, symbolises the eight Beatitudes (as listed in Christ's Sermon on the Mount), and also the eight *langues* of the Order of St John: Allemagne (Germany), Aragon (Spain), Auvergne, Castille, England, France, Italy and Provence.

The four main sections of the cross symbolise the four Cardinal Virtues (Fortitude, Justice, Temperance and Perseverance). The Knights of St John were bound by monastic vows, and they observed the obligations of poverty, chastity and obedience.

century. Each one differed in scale and style, reflecting the wealth of the Knights and the progressive gusto with which Cassar worked.

The wealthiest of the Knights had their own lodgings, but dining in their *auberge* four times a week was compulsory. This presumably was no hardship since the *auberges* were well known for their high culinary standards. According to a 17th-century French writer, 'partridges, pigeons, rabbits, thrushes, and other game (in Malta) are fatter than anywhere else in Europe'.

Of the *auberges* no longer in existence, the Auberge d'Allemagne (*Pjazza Indipendenza/Independence Square*) was pulled down to make way for St Paul's Anglican Cathedral; the Auberge d'Auvergne (*Triq ir-Repubblika/Republic Street*) was bombed in 1942 and replaced by the new Law Courts; and the Auberge de France (*Triq Nofs-in-Nhar/South Street*) was replaced by the General Workers' Union headquarters.

Auberge d'Angleterre et de Bavière

Overlooking Marsamxett Harbour, this was originally the Palazzo Carnerio. It did not become the *auberge* of the Anglo-Bavarian *langue* until 1784, and only existed as such for 15 years. Among the surviving *auberges*, this one is the least impressive.
On the English Curtain section of Triq San Bastjan (Bastion Rd). Not open to the public.

Auberge d'Aragon

Built in 1571, this is the oldest and simplest of the *auberges*, a plain single-storey building facing St Paul's

Cassar's Renaissance-style Auberge d'Italie is now the Ministry for Tourism and Culture

Anglican Cathedral. It is now used by the government for their offices.
Pjazza Indipendenza (Independence Square). Not open to the public.

Auberge de Castille et Léon

Originally designed by Cassar, the *auberge* was remodelled in 1744 for the Portuguese Grand Master Pinto. This libertine loved pomp and grandeur; of all the *auberges* (and arguably, all the 18th-century buildings in Malta), this is the most magnificent.

It is also the most Italianate, based on the Baroque architecture of Lecce in southern Italy. A flamboyant bust of Pinto, surrounded by trophies, banners and arms, adorns the façade. Once the headquarters of the British Army, the building has now become the prime minister's office.
Pjazza Kastilja (Castille Place). Not open to the public.

Auberge d'Italie

Now housing the Ministry for Tourism and Culture and the Malta Tourism Authority, the Auberge d'Italie has been substantially altered and enlarged since it was built in the late 16th century. It is typical of Cassar's work in its rustication and carved quoins.
Triq il-Merkanti (Merchants' St). Not open to the public.

Auberge de Provence

Founded in 1571, this *auberge* now houses the National Museum of Archaeology (*see p42*). It was the most

lavish *auberge* of them all, renowned for the excellence of its cuisine and its ornately decorated rooms. The rich façade, possibly remodelled in the 17th century, is fronted by both Doric and Ionic columns.
Triq ir-Repubblika (Republic St). Admission charge.

THE CHURCHES

The Knights of St John, who combined the careers of monk and soldier, were responsible for most of Valletta's churches. Some of the best are described below; the greatest, St John's Co-Cathedral, is covered on *pp34–7*.

Carmelite Church

The massive dome of the Carmelite Church, which rivals the nearby spire of the Anglican cathedral, is a dominant (and much-criticised) feature of the Valletta skyline. Originally built in 1573 by Gerolamo Cassar, after the devastation of World War II a new structure of far larger proportions was built around the old church. The interior is huge: light, spacious and unusually free of elaborate ornamentation.
Triq it-Teatru il-Qadim (Old Theatre St). Open: Mon–Fri 9am–noon & 5–7pm. Free admission.

Church of Gesù

Dating from the late 16th century, this ornate church was built in conjunction with the Jesuit College. When the Jesuits were thrown off the island in 1768, the college became the University

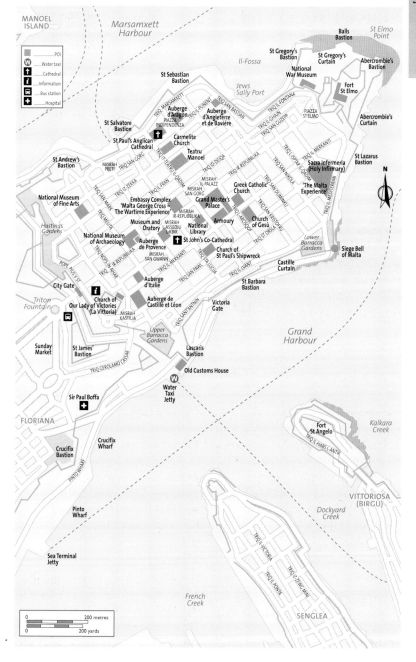

MANOEL ISLAND

Marsamxett Harbour

Balls Bastion

St Elmo Point

St Gregory's Bastion

St Gregory's Curtain

Abercrombie's Bastion

Il-Fossa

National War Museum

St Sebastian Bastion

Jews Sally Port

Fort St Elmo

POI

Water taxi

Cathedral

Information

Bus station

Hospital

St Salvatore Bastion

Auberge d'Aragon

PIAZZA INDIPENDENZA

TRIQ MARSAMXETT

TRIQ IL-PUNENT

Auberge d'Angleterre et de Bavière

TRIQ SAN BASTJAN

TRIQ IL-GHAN

TRIQ SAN GIŻEP

PIAZZA ST ELMO

Abercrombie's Curtain

St Paul's Anglican Cathedral

Carmelite Church

Teatru Manoel

TRIQ IT-TEATRU L-QADIM

TRIQ ID-DEJQA

TRIQ IR-REPUBBLIKA

TRIQ L-ISPTAR IL-QADIM

TRIQ SAN NIKOLA

Sacra Infermeria (Holy Infirmary)

St Lazarus Bastion

St Andrew's Bastion

MISRAH PRETI

TRIQ SAN GORG

TRIQ IZ-ZEKKA

TRIQ IL-FRAN

MISRAH IL-PALAZZ

MISRAH SAN GORG

Greek Catholic Church

TRIQ SAN DUMINU

'The Malta Experience'

National Museum of Fine Arts

TRIQ MELITA

TRIQ SAN MARK

Embassy Complex 'Malta George Cross – The Wartime Experience'

MISRAH IR-REPUBBLIKA

Grand Master's Palace

TRIQ L-ARCISQOF

TRIQ SAN ĠUSTINU

Church of Ġesù

Hastings Gardens

Museum and Oratory

MISRAH L-ASSEDJU L-KBIR

National Library

Armoury

National Museum of Archaeology

TRIQ NOFS IN-NHAR

TRIQ IR-REPUBBLIKA

Auberge de Provence

St John's Co-Cathedral

TRIQ ŠT ORSLA

POPE PIUS ST

MISRAH SAN ĠWANN

Church of St Paul's Shipwreck

Lower Barracca Gardens

Siege Bell of Malta

Auberge d'Italie

TRIQ IL-MERKANTI

TRIQ SAN PAWL

TRIQ SANTA LUCIJA

Castille Curtain

City Gate

Triton Fountain

Church of Our Lady of Victories (La Vittoria)

MISRAH KASTILJA

Auberge de Castille et Léon

TRIQ SANT'ANTNIN

TRIQ L-LVANT

Victoria Gate

St Barbara Bastion

Grand Harbour

Sunday Market

St James' Bastion

TRIQ GEROLAMO CASSAR

Upper Barracca Gardens

Lascaris Bastion

Old Customs House

Water Taxi Jetty

Sir Paul Boffa

FLORIANA

Fort St Angelo

Kalkara Creek

TRIQ IL-ĦABS L-ANTIK

Crucifix Bastion

Crucifix Wharf

PINTO WHARF

Dockyard Creek

VITTORIOSA (BIRGU)

Pinto Wharf

TRIQ VICTORIA

TRIQ IL-PONTA

TRIQ IZ-ZEWĠ MINI

Sea Terminal Jetty

French Creek

SENGLEA

0   200 metres

0   200 yards

of Malta and this is now its church, worth a visit for the paintings and carvings.

Triq il-Merkanti (Merchants' St). Open: Mon–Fri 9am–noon & 5–7pm. Free admission.

Church of Our Lady of Victories (La Vittoria)

This is the oldest building in Valletta, built to commemorate the Knights' victory in the Great Siege of 1565. Grand Master La Valette laid the foundation stone in 1566 and – according to his wishes – was later buried in the church. His body was eventually moved to the crypt of the Co-Cathedral where many Grand Masters were subsequently buried. Our Lady of Victories was redesigned in Baroque style in the 17th century, and a bell tower was added in 1752.

The two houses next to the church, distinguished by the fat mouldings on the windows and the ceramic tiling, are two of the very oldest houses in the city. The smaller one belonged to the priest.

Triq Nofs-in-Nhar (South St). Open: Mon–Sat 8.30am–1pm. Free admission.

Church of St Paul's Shipwreck

This is one of the oldest and most elaborate of the city's churches, its interior richly endowed with coloured marble and gilded woodwork. The vault is decorated with frescoes of scenes from the life of St Paul. The church also possesses a finely carved wooden statue of St Paul, which is ceremoniously carried aloft through the streets of Valletta on 10 February, the Feast of St Paul's Shipwreck (*see p24*).

Triq San Pawl (St Paul's St). Open: Mon–Fri 9am–7pm. Free admission.

Greek Catholic Church

The church contains a 12th-century icon which is said to have been brought by the Knights from the island of Rhodes in the 16th century.

Triq l-Arċisqof (Archbishop St). Open: Mon–Sat 7.30–10am, Sun & public holidays 5–10am. Free admission.

St John's Co-Cathedral

The simple, sober façade of St John's gives no hint of its lavish interior. It was built as the main church of the Order, and the Knights spent enormous sums of money embellishing the chapels of their *langues*. Almost every last piece of the walls, vault and chapels is painted, gilded or carved. Knights and Grand Masters are omnipresent in the form of their heraldic arms, monuments and mausoleums. The *pavimento* (floor paving) consists of numerous multicoloured marble tombstones, bearing – along with carvings of skeletons and symbols of death – the names and shields of past members of the Order.

The cathedral was built between 1572 and 1581 by Gerolamo Cassar, and his training as a military engineer accounts for the sober exterior. Nearly a century later the prolific Italian artist Mattia Preti transformed Cassar's severe interior into a glowing showpiece of Baroque art. His greatest task, which occupied him for five years, was the decoration of the vault, which features a narrative cycle depicting the life of St John the Baptist.

Chapels

Each of the side chapels belonged to the *langues*. They are variously decorated, but their characteristic features are the symbols of the individual *langues*, and the arms of the various Grand Masters. Preti's paintings decorate many of the chapels; worth singling out are *St George and the Dragon* in the Chapel of Aragon, and the serene *Mystical Marriage of St Catherine* in the Chapel of Italy. The monuments to the Grand Masters are works of art in their own right, the very finest being the richly decorated marble and bronze mausoleums to Grand Masters Nicolas Cotoner and Ramon Perellos in the Chapel of Aragon, Catalonia and Navarre.

The beautiful dome of the Carmelite Church, Valletta

The measured façade of St John's
Co-Cathedral, designed by a military architect

painting *The Beheading of St John the Baptist*. This huge, vigorous work of art dominates the oratory. Also by Caravaggio is the painting of *St Jerome* on the opposite wall.

The highlights of the museum are the splendid Belgian tapestries which are based on paintings by Poussin and Rubens. During June, the month of the *festa* of St John, the tapestries are brought out of the museum to adorn the interior of the church where they can be seen by all who visit the church. *Entrance and ticket office on Triq ir-Repubblika (Republic St). Tel: (356) 21220536. www.stjohnscocathedral.com. Open: Mon–Fri 9.30am–4.30pm (last admission 4pm), Sat 9.30am–12.30pm (last admission noon). Closed: Sun &*

Crypt of the Grand Masters

The remains of 12 Grand Masters are buried here, mostly in sarcophagi. The only ordinary Knight who was buried in the crypt is Sir Oliver Starkey, English secretary to the French Grand Master Jean Parisot de la Valette during the Great Siege of 1565.

Museum and Oratory

Of all the artistic treasures in the church, the *pièce de résistance* is generally considered to be Caravaggio's

CARAVAGGIO

Michelangelo Merisi was known as Caravaggio, after the town near Milan where he was born in 1573. One of the most revolutionary painters of his day, he founded a school of painting based on realism heightened by the use of *chiaroscuro* (light and shade). Notorious for his violent temper, his career in Rome came to a sudden end when he stabbed a man during a game of racquets and was forced to flee to Naples.

In 1608 he came to Malta and painted a portrait of the Grand Master Wignacourt. As a reward, he was made a Knight of the Order, and was commissioned to paint the two works that can still be seen in St John's Co-Cathedral. However, another enraged attack, this time on one of the most senior Knights, led to his imprisonment. He escaped and fled to Syracuse, but died in 1610 at Porto Ercole on the Tuscan coast.

*public holidays. Admission charge
(includes audio guide). No stiletto heels
(slippers can be purchased at the
ticket desk).*

St Paul's Anglican Cathedral

Dowager Queen Adelaide, widow of
Britain's King William IV, visited Malta
during the winter of 1838–39, and was
so appalled at the lack of an Anglican
church in Valletta that she decided to

Inside, the Co-Cathedral is resplendent with
tapestries and wall paintings

pay for one to be built. The cathedral
was designed in classical style, complete
with a Gothic spire which soars 65m
(213ft) above the city.
*Pjazza Indipendenza (Independence
Square). Open: Mon–Sat 9am–5pm.
Free admission.*

GRAND MASTER'S PALACE

The 18th-century Scottish traveller
Patrick Brydone noted that 'the
Grand Master (who studies conveniency
more than magnificence) is more
comfortably and commodiously lodged
than any prince in Europe, the King of
Sardinia perhaps only excepted'.
Behind its inappropriately severe
façade, and in spite of the malicious
pillaging by Napoleon's troops
following the French occupation in
1798, the palace still conveys an
impression of the splendour to which
the Grand Masters were accustomed.

Converted from a smaller house,
the palace was designed by Gerolamo
Cassar in 1571. From the time of its
completion until the end of the
Order's reign in Malta (1798), the
palace was used by all the Grand
Masters. In 1800 it became the
official residence of the British
governors. The palace is now the
presidential office, and also Malta's
Parliament House.

The two courtyards originally
formed one large area. Neptune's
Court, in the centre, is named after a
bronze statue of the sea god, standing
among greenery, which is said to have

been rescued from the old fish market in the 17th century. Prince Alfred's Court is smaller, planted with palms, pittosporum and a charming jacaranda tree. On the elaborate clock tower four bronze figurines of Moorish slaves strike the hours.

Armoury

Only about a quarter of the arms and armour belonging to the Knights has survived, but it is still a formidable collection, with around 6,000 pieces in all. Among them are daggers, rapiers, halberds, cannon, pistols and some stunningly decorated suits of armour. In one room rows of Knights in armour stand to attention, while the special suits of armour individually made for the Grand Masters are displayed separately. The most splendid of these is the suit inlaid with gold made for Grand Master Wignacourt in 1610–20. Among the weapons and armoury of the Knights' adversaries are Turkish battle axes, helmets, gilded shields and a sword said to have belonged to the corsair Dragut.
Open: daily 9am–5pm.
Admission charge (includes audio guide).

The exterior of the Grand Master's Palace betrays nothing of the splendour within

State rooms

Short guided tours take place at regular intervals, provided that the state rooms are not in use. Visits start in the Tapestry Chamber, originally the Council Chamber of the Knights. The walls here are hung with stunning Gobelin tapestries, featuring tropical scenes set in South America, the Caribbean, India and Africa. The tapestries, though nearly three centuries old, look as good as new, and were given to the Order by Grand Master Ramon Perellos in 1710.

Of all the rooms, the most magnificent is the Hall of St Michael and St George, also known as the Throne Room, decorated with a cycle of 12 frescoes, vividly portraying the 1565 Siege of Malta. The artist was Matteo Perez d'Aleccio, an engraver and painter who had once helped Michelangelo with the Sistine Chapel.

These detailed scenes start with the Fall of St Elmo on 23 June 1565, and end with the departure of the Turkish fleet from Malta on 8 September. Opposite the throne there is a charming gallery made from the stern of the great carrack, the *Santa Maria*, in which the Grand Master de l'Isle-Adam sailed away from the island of Rhodes in 1522, fleeing the terrible forces of Suleiman the Magnificent.

Leading off the Hall of St Michael and St George, the State Dining Room has magnificent 17th-century chandeliers and portraits of British monarchs, from King George III to Queen Elizabeth II.

The Hall of the Ambassadors was originally the Grand Master's audience chamber. Known also as the Red Room, it is decorated in crimson with Louis XV furniture, and a high frieze recalling episodes from the early history of the Order when it still had bases in Jerusalem, Cyprus and Rhodes.

Triq il-Merkanti (Merchants' St), Misrah il-Palazz (Palace Square). Tel: (356) 21249349. Open: daily 9am–5pm. State rooms open: Fri–Wed 10am–4pm. Admission charge.

MUSEUMS AND OTHER ATTRACTIONS
'Malta George Cross – The Wartime Experience'

This 45-minute audiovisual show combines stills, films and Sensurround sound systems to tell the story of the Siege of 1942.

Embassy Complex, Triq Sta Lucia (St Lucy St). Tel: (356) 21227436. Shows daily on the hour 10am–1pm. Admission charge.

National Library

Also known as the Bibliotheca, this imposing building dominates Republic Square. Built in the late 18th century, it is the repository of a large number of original documents recording the administration of the Order of St John. The original library was built by the

(*Cont. on p42*)

The Knights of St John

The Knights of the Order of St John of Jerusalem (to give their full name) were formed long before their reign in Malta. The Order was originally established in 1085 as a community of monks responsible for looking after the sick at the Hospital of St John in Jerusalem. They later became a military order, defending crusader territory in the Holy Lands, and safeguarding the perilous routes

A Knight in armour

taken by medieval pilgrims. The Knights were drawn exclusively from noble families, and the Order acquired vast wealth from those it recruited, as well as from the ill-gotten gains of their subsequent privateering.

The Knights came to Malta in 1530, having been ejected from their earlier home on Rhodes by the Turks in 1522. Charles V, the Holy Roman Emperor, gave them the choice of Malta or Tripoli as a new base. Neither was to their liking, but they thought, on the other hand, that nothing could be worse than Tripoli.

Having chosen Malta, the Knights stayed for 268 years, transforming what they called 'merely a rock of soft sandstone' into a flourishing island with mighty defences, and a capital city coveted by the great powers of Europe.

The Order was ruled by a Grand Master who was answerable only to the Pope. Knights were chosen from the aristocratic families of France, Italy, Spain, England and Portugal. On acceptance into the Order they were sworn to celibacy, poverty and obedience. Few of the Knights lived up to these ideals; many of them were very wealthy, and their standoffish attitude towards the locals

Caravaggio's painting *The Beheading of St John the Baptist*, in the oratory of the lavish St John's Co-Cathedral

does not seem to have applied when it came to the temptations of the flesh.

Ironically, it was the two great victories of the Knights which spelt the death knell of the Order. The Great Siege of 1565, followed by the crucial Battle of Lepanto in 1571, were both so successful in checking the Ottoman advance into the western Mediterranean that there was no longer an Infidel to fight. The Order gradually grew complacent and corrupt and the Knights had little to do but scour the seas for booty from Muslim ships.

By the late 18th century the Order was little more than a large but effete international gentlemen's club. The island was ripe for picking by Napoleon in 1798. When, four years later, the Order was formally restored to Malta, the Maltese resisted their return, and sought British protection.

Knights in 1555. From 1612 the sale of any book belonging to deceased Knights was forbidden, hence this vast collection of valuable leather-bound tomes. Among the documents is the letter in which Henry VIII proclaims himself Head of the Church of England.

Misrah ir-Repubblika (Republic Square). Tel: (356) 21236585. Email: customercare.nlm@gov.mt. Open: mid-Jun–Sept Mon–Sat 8.15am–1.15pm; off season Mon–Fri 8.15am–5pm, Sat 8.15am–1.15pm. Free admission.

National Museum of Archaeology

For anyone remotely interested in prehistory, this rich repository of Malta's archaeological treasures is essential viewing. If you have already seen Malta's temples and tombs, the museum will be doubly rewarding because it contains many archaeological finds taken from those sites for preservation. If you have not yet seen them, a tour of the museum should fire your enthusiasm to visit at least the major prehistoric sites.

Exhibits aside, the museum has the privilege of occupying the only *auberge* open to the public. One of the more luxurious, the Auberge de Provence (*see p32*) was designed in 1571 by Gerolamo Cassar for the Knights of the *langue* of Provence. The ground-floor display, with remarkable finds from the Neolithic and Temple periods (*see p12*), has undergone major refurbishment. Exhibits are well displayed behind glass cabinets, with

excellent English labelling, and there are superb small-scale reconstructions of the temple complexes.

The pieces include flints, pottery, human skulls, necklaces and modern-looking obese female statuettes. Among the highlights are discoveries from the Ħal Saflieni Hypogeum underground burial site, such as the *Sleeping Lady*. Also here is the fat, headless *Venus of Malta* from Ħaġar Qim.

The Tarxien section has a wealth of treasures from the Tarxien temples, including pots and vases (which have been painstakingly reassembled), carbonised seeds and grasses found in cinerary urns, and the lower half of the famous fat fertility goddess. You can also see decorative blocks (removed from the temples and replaced by replicas) ornamented with elaborate spiral motifs and dating from 3000–2500 BC.

The first floor, or *piano nobile*, covers the Bronze Age, Punic, Classical, Arab, medieval and Baroque periods.

Auberge de Provence, Triq ir-Repubblika (Republic St). Tel: (356) 21239375. www.heritagemalta.org. Open: daily 9am–7pm. Admission charge.

National Museum of Fine Arts

This art collection occupies three floors of a fine Baroque *palazzo* that was built by the Knights in the 16th century and remodelled in the 18th century. For many years the building served as the official residence of the commander-in-chief of the British fleet, during which time it was commonly known as Admiralty House.

The highlights are the Baroque paintings by Mattia Preti, and the sculpture on the first floor by Antonio Sciortino (1879–1940), who was obsessed with the theme of dynamic movement – wonderfully illustrated in his cast of *Speed*. Room 8 features *Christ the Redeemer*, painted by Guido Reni, which once hung in the private suite of the Grand Master's Palace. Rooms 8 to 11 contain a series of large and striking canvases in the style of Caravaggio.

Rooms 12 and 13 are devoted to the work of Mattia Preti (1613–99), who transformed St John's Co-Cathedral (*see pp34–7*) into a blazing monument to the glory of the Order. Preti originally came from Calabria, but moved to Malta in 1661 to decorate the cathedral. He was made a Knight and spent the last 40 years of his life here. His paintings, full of movement and scenic effects, demonstrate the strong influences of Caravaggio and – in their colouring – of the Venetian artists of the late 16th century.

The ground-floor rooms are devoted to 18th-century French and Italian painters, in addition to a section on modern Maltese art. The highlight of the 19th-century collection, in Room 18, is Turner's watercolour of the Grand Harbour (1830).

In the basement there is a fascinating collection of memorabilia of the Order, including portraits of dignitaries,

ceramics and silverware from the Sacra Infermeria (*see pp44–6*).
Triq Nofs-in-Nhar (South St).
Tel: (356) 22954341. Open: daily
9am–5pm. Admission charge.

National War Museum

Fort St Elmo is famous for its role in the epic Siege of 1565 and, more recently, for its role in World War II; it thus makes a fitting home for Malta's National War Museum. The war relics shown here date from the year 1798, but the main emphasis is on World War II.

The chief exhibits are displayed in the main hall: an Italian E-boat, flanked by two World War I German torpedoes, Italian and German anti-tank guns, and

The ample torso of a female statuette excavated at Ħaġar Qim

Assorted items of military hardware in the National War Museum in Fort St Elmo

the aircraft *Faith* – sole survivor of Malta's tiny air force, made up of just three Gloster Gladiators (*Faith, Hope* and *Charity*). In an alcove is the George Cross awarded to Malta by King George VI on 15 April 1942.

Photographs taken during World War II serve as a chilling reminder of the devastation caused to Malta by German bombardments, and of the dire conditions suffered by servicemen and civilians. Among the other exhibits are wrecked aircraft raised from the seabed and relics of the destroyers sunk in the Grand Harbour, in addition to displays of battledress and gas masks. *Fort St Elmo. Tel: (356) 21222430. War Museum open: daily 9am–5pm. Fort St Elmo is accessible only for military re-enactments (see pp154–5).*

Sacra Infermeria (Holy Infirmary)

Wherever the Knights set up a base they built a hospital, and Malta was no exception. The Sacra Infermeria, begun in 1574, had the longest hospital ward in the world (155m/170yds), and acquired international fame for its equipment and high medical standards. In the 17th century it was described as having 'one of the grandest interiors in the world'. Patients were fed from silver plates, and were looked after by novices, by the Knights, and sometimes even by the Grand Master himself.

The Order was obliged to take in the sick, the destitute and the insane, regardless of their religion. Protestants, Muslims and members of the Greek Orthodox Church were, however, put in a separate ward. For many years the only privilege a sick Knight could claim was two sheets instead of one. However, by the 17th century, many members of the Order had their own rooms, and were soon to be the only patients who were allowed to eat off silver platters.

When the Order was ousted from Malta, Napoleon threw out the patients, looted the silver and then melted it down to pay the troops who had taken part in his Egyptian campaign.

Under British rule, the Sacra Infermeria became a military hospital, and part was used as stables. The building was badly damaged during World War II, although this did not stop it being used by the troops for social occasions. The grand reopening, this time as a conference centre, took place in 1979. The expert restoration won it the Europa Nostra Award. Tragically, the main hall was destroyed

by fire in 1987, but it was rebuilt. The conference centre features the Knights Hospitallers' exhibition, and the audiovisual show 'The Malta Experience' (*see below*).
Triq il-Mediterran (Mediterranean St).
Tel: (356) 21243840.
Conference centre open: Mon–Fri
9am–4.30pm.
'Knights Hospitallers' open: Sat–Sun
9.30am–4pm. Admission charge.

'The Malta Experience'

Appropriately located in the converted hospital of the Order of St John, this

The National Museum of Fine Arts is housed in a former Admiralty building

multivision show highlights 7,000 years of Maltese history – from Neolithic origins to the modern day. Some 3,000 colour slides, high-tech sound effects and a lively commentary combine to make this an easy, entertaining way to acquire a basic knowledge of Malta's complex past.

The entrance is next to Fort St Elmo, on Mediterranean St, on the lower floor of the Mediterranean Conference Centre. Tel: (356) 21243776. Email: info@themaltaexperience.com. www.themaltaexperience.com. Shows last 45 minutes, Mon–Fri every hour, 11am–4pm, Sat–Sun & public holidays 11am–1pm. From October to June there is an additional screening at 2pm at weekends and on public holidays. Admission charge.

Teatru Manoel

This gem of a theatre is said to be the third oldest in Europe. It was built in 1731 by the Portuguese Grand Master, Manoel de Vilhena, 'for the honest entertainment of the people'. The religious life to which the Knights were committed did not stop them indulging in theatrical pursuits. Watching or participating in pageants, operas and plays was very much part of their life.

The Manoel has had a chequered history and, after a flourishing beginning, it was variously used as a doss house, dance hall and cinema. During the 1860s, thanks to the enlarged garrison and fleet, and an

THE GEORGE CROSS

The George Cross was instituted by the British king George VI 'for acts of the greatest heroism or of the most conspicuous courage in circumstances of extreme danger'. Malta is the only nation to have been awarded the medal. The award of the medal is explained in a letter of 15 April 1942 sent from Buckingham Palace to the Governor of Malta: 'To honour her brave people I award the George Cross to the Island Fortress of Malta to bear witness to a heroism and devotion that will long be famous in history.'

To commemorate the 50th anniversary of the award, Queen Elizabeth II and the Duke of Edinburgh visited Malta in 1992.

increase in the number of visitors to Malta, the theatre was declared inadequate, and sold to finance the building of the new Royal Opera House in Valletta. It was not until the Opera House was laid to ruins in World War II that the Manoel came to life again. In response to a public appeal the Maltese government acquired the building, and experts from Britain and Italy were called in to supervise its restoration. The glorious ceiling, with its 22-carat gold gilding, and the tiny *paysages* (rural scenes) on the boxes were all restored to their original splendour.

In December 1960 the grand reopening was celebrated by the Ballet Rambert's performance of *Coppelia*. Since then the theatre has never looked back. The Bonici Palace adjoining the theatre has also been restored to form the theatre foyer.

The small museum, which is covered on guided tours, contains a collection of costumes, portraits, drawings, stage designs and other theatre memorabilia.

Triq it-Teatru il-Qadim (Old Theatre St). Tel: (356) 21246389. www.teatrumanoel.com.mt. Guided tours every 45 minutes: Mon–Fri 10.30am–3pm, Sat 10.15am–12.30pm. Admission charge.

The Valletta Waterfront

Below the bastions of Pinto Wharf, the splendid old warehouses built by the Knights have been restored and converted to brasseries and cafés with spacious open-air terraces. Providing there is no huge cruiser blocking your views (this is also the site of the sea terminal jetty) you can enjoy looking across the Grand Harbour to the Three Cities (and the cranes of Senglea).

The Teatru Manoel, restored to its former glory

Cruise: Valletta harbour

Taking a cruise around Malta's two great harbours will give you a fascinating insight into the island's long history. The cruiser weaves in and out of every creek, providing views of Valletta's bastions, forts and docks. You will also see numerous boats, ranging from enormous cruisers and ocean-going tankers, to tiny, brightly painted fishing boats.

The cruiser heads south across Sliema Creek; the dome of the Carmelite Church, and the spire of St Paul's Anglican Cathedral dominate the Valletta skyline.

Manoel Island

Fort Manoel, built in 1726 by the Knights as a garrison for 500 men, and Lazzaretto di San Rocco, created as a quarantine station, are both part of the Tigné Point Development (*see pp57–8*). The project is part residential, part commercial and will include dining and leisure facilities.

The boat skirts Lazzaretto Creek, which, with Msida Creek, is Malta's major yachting marina. It then rounds the promontory of Ta'Xbiex, where several embassies occupy large mansions, before entering Msida Creek.

The *Black Pearl*

At the head of Msida Creek, the *Black Pearl* was a Swedish brigantine which caught fire in the Suez Canal and was abandoned in Marsamxett Harbour.

She was brought to life again for use in the film *Popeye*, shot at Anchor Bay in Malta (*see p115*). More recently she has been used as a restaurant.

Cruising across to Pietà Creek, the boat passes Gwardamanġa Hill, where Princess Elizabeth (later Queen Elizabeth II) stayed as a guest of Lord Mountbatten when Prince Philip was stationed in Malta. From here the boat plies across the harbour towards the open sea, skirting the great fortifications of Floriana and Valletta.

Grand Harbour

This great natural harbour, with its sheltered anchorages and creeks, has been coveted by many a foreign fleet. Fort St Elmo, to the right, and Ricasoli Fort, to the left, guard both sides of the harbour entrance.

As you cruise along the eastern side of Valletta, look out for the main landmarks (*described in more detail on pp52–3*). After Fort St Elmo, you will see the memorial Siege Bell of Malta,

BOAT TOURS

In fair weather, various cruise boats depart several times a day from Sliema Ferries. The smaller **Luzzu Cruises** can penetrate all the inlets. The tour lasts 90 minutes (*tel: (356) 79064489*). There is also **Captain Morgan Cruises** (*Tel: (356) 23463333. Email: info@captainmorgan.com.mt*).

followed by the Lower and Upper Barracca Gardens. Skirting the eastern defences of Floriana, the cruiser then heads into Marsa Creek, which, with its huge cranes and tankers, its shipyard and power station, is the most industrialised part of the harbour. *From here the boat turns round to explore the creeks and dockyards of the Three Cities on the opposite side of the harbour.*

Dockyards and creeks

The Knights established the first dockyard here in Malta's Grand Harbour. The dry docks date back to 1804. By 1938 the number of dockyard workers here reached 12,000; today, the number is around 5,000, mostly employed in ship-repair work. French Creek, the next inlet, affords good views of repair docks and the tightly packed flat-topped houses of Senglea.

Rounding the tip of Senglea Peninsula, where a stone *vedette* (lookout post) carved with an eye and an ear keeps watch over the harbour, the boat enters Dockyard Creek. Fort St Angelo occupies the tip of the next promontory. During the siege, the Knights strung a chain from the base of the fort to the shore of Senglea in order to keep the Turks out. Further into Dockyard Creek, the large twin-belfried Church of St Lawrence overlooks the waterfront.

Between the next two inlets, Kalkara and Rinella Creeks, you will see a graceful classical building, which was formerly a hospital. The boat exits the harbour past the semi-derelict Ricasoli Fort – setting of *Troy*, *Gladiator* and other blockbusters – and returns to Sliema via St Elmo and the Tigné Peninsula.

Cruise: Valletta harbour

Cruising in Valletta harbour

Walk: Valletta

This stroll takes you through the heart of the city, past churches, palaces, auberges and a lot of modern shopfronts. Avoid Saturday afternoon and Sunday, when the streets lack their characteristic bustle.

Allow 1 hour.

Start at City Gate.

1 Royal Opera House

From City Gate you enter Freedom Square where you will see the sad ruins of the Royal Opera House, once a splendid venue for theatre and opera. No attempt has been made to reverse the devastation of World War II, and opera performances now take place in the Teatru Manoel (*see pp46–7*).

2 Triq ir-Repubblika

Straight ahead of you is Triq ir-Repubblika, the city's main artery, bustling by day with workers, shoppers and tourists, and in the evening with locals out for the *passiġġata* (promenade). A short way down on the left, the Auberge de Provence houses the National Museum of Archaeology (*see p42*).
The next right turn takes you to St John's Square and the façade of St John's Co-Cathedral (see pp34–7). The entrance is back on Republic St.

3 Misrah L-Assedju L-Kbir

On Great Siege Square the allegorical monument, commemorating those who died in the Great Siege of 1565, is by the Maltese sculptor Antonio Sciortino (1879–1947). Across the road, the Law Courts occupy an imposing modern building in classical style.

4 Misrah ir-Repubblika

A few steps further on will bring you to the tree-lined Misrah ir-Repubblika, presided over by a statue of Queen Victoria.
Immediately after the square turn left down Triq it-Teatru il-Qadim (Old Theatre St). Stop at the first street.

5 Triq id-Dejqa

The very narrow Strait Street was the only place where the Knights were allowed to fight duels.
Walk to the end of Triq it-Teatru il-Qadim, passing the Teatru Manoel

(see pp46–7), *the Carmelite Church
(see p32), and various little grocery
shops and bars. Note the plaque to Sir
Walter Scott, who stayed in the building
on the left when it was a hotel. Turn
right for Pjazza Indipendenza
(Independence Square), overlooked by
St Paul's Anglican Cathedral (see p37),
then return to Triq ir-Repubblika via
Triq l-Arċisqof (Archbishop St). At
Misrah il-Palazz (Palace Square), turn
left down towards the steepest part of
Triq ir-Repubblika.*

6 Casa Rocca Piccola

The small, late 16th-century *palazzo*
at No 74 provides a rare opportunity
to visit a historic home still occupied
by a Maltese noble family and a
World War II bomb shelter.
*Guided tours Mon–Sat, on the hour
10am–4pm. Admission charge.
Walk down to Fort St Elmo,
turn right, then right again for
Triq il-Merkanti.*

7 Triq il-Merkanti

The aptly named Merchants' Street is
lined with small neighbourhood stores
and tailors, as well as Baroque churches
and *palazzi*. There is a bustling
morning market.
*A right turn at the end of the street,
passing La Vittoria church on your
left (see p34), will bring you back to
the start.*

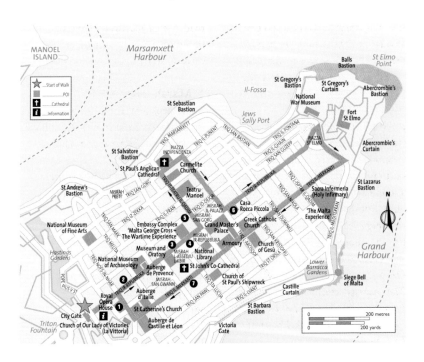

Walk: Valletta's ramparts

Sense the excitement of the past as you walk along the mighty Valletta ramparts and overlook the great harbour where famous battles were fought. The Knights' defensive system of bastions, curtains and forts was one of history's most remarkable military architectural feats.

The round circuit takes about 2 hours, allowing for stops.

Start at City Gate. Just inside on your left a stairway takes you up to Pope Pius V St, above the ramparts. Turn right for Hastings Gardens.

1 Hastings Gardens

Forming part of the St John and St Michael Bastions, these gardens protect the rear of the city at the highest point of Mount Sceberras. Stop here for views of Floriana and Marsamxett Harbour.

Leaving the gardens, bear right. Ahead you will see the lofty steeple of St Paul's Anglican Cathedral and the large dome of the Carmelite Church. Beyond St Andrew's Bastion, continue along the street and descend the Biagio Steps. Carry on to St Sebastian Bastion.

2 St Sebastian Bastion

Stop here to admire the views across to Manoel Island, fortified by Grand Master de Vilhena between 1723 and 1732.

Carry on above the English and French Curtains, both named after the langues

whose duty it was to defend them, to reach Fort St Elmo.

3 Fort St Elmo

Occupying the vulnerable extremity of the Valletta promontory, this fort bore the brunt of the Turkish bombardments in the 1565 Siege (*see pp16–17*). Rebuilt after the Siege and altered over the centuries, the fort can only be visited for military re-enactments (*see pp154–5*) but the National War Museum is open daily (*see pp43–4*).

On the far side of the fort, follow the ramparts along St Lazarus Bastion for panoramic views of the Grand Harbour. On the landward side is the Sacra Infermeria (*see pp44–6*).

Make for the large harbourside bell.

4 Siege Bell of Malta

This bronze bell commemorates the 8,000 British and Maltese who fell in the 1940–43 Siege of Malta, and was unveiled by Queen Elizabeth II and the president of Malta on 29 May 1992.

Follow Triq il-Mediterran (Mediterranean St) as it forks right, then turn left into the Lower Barracca Gardens.

5 Lower Barracca Gardens

The temple commemorates Sir Alexander Ball, the British captain who assisted the Maltese in their uprising against the French in 1798.
Follow St Barbara Bastion (not signed), and turn left again at the end of St Lucy Curtain. Turn left at the end for Victoria Gate and down to the bastion.

6 Lascaris Bastion

Named after the Grand Master, the bastion houses the Lascaris War Rooms, where the island's defensive strategies were planned in the last World War.
Return to Victoria Gate and take the steps up to Upper Barracca Gardens.

7 Upper Barracca Gardens

These gardens command a spectacular panorama across the Grand Harbour to the Three Cities. A midday gun is still fired daily at the old Saluting Battery, below the balcony.
Turn inland to Pjazza Kastilja (Castille Place) overlooked by the Auberge de Castille et Léon. Cross to St James' Bastion, where the dry moat below is the scene of the Sunday-morning market. The 'Valletta Centre' road will bring you back to your starting point above City Gate.

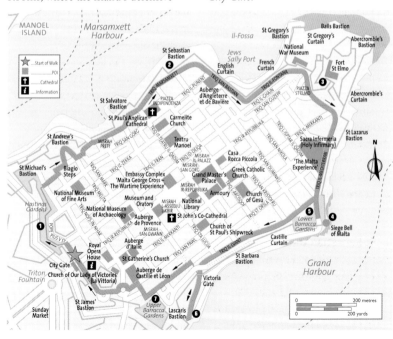

Valletta environs

Richly decorated churches are the highlights of Valletta's traffic-choked conurbation. Floriana, a suburban extension of Valletta, has recently been enlivened by the Pinto Wharf development – otherwise known as the Valletta Waterfront (see p47). This combines a cruise ship and seaplane terminal with an appealing waterfront of restaurants, cafés and shops.

Birkirkara

The old centre, with its narrow streets and ancient residences, still has something of the look of a traditional Maltese village. The main interest lies in the churches. **St Helena's** is one of the island's biggest and richest churches, its spacious interior elaborately gilded and painted. It is also home to Malta's largest bell.

The **Church of the Annunciation**, built by Vittorio Cassar (son of the more famous Gerolamo), is an interesting example of Maltese Renaissance architecture, with more than a hint of Spanish in the façade. Most recent of all is the sanctuary erected by the Carmelite Fathers which lies on the edge of town.

Floriana

The suburb of Floriana was built in 1634 to extend the fortifications of Valletta in the event of renewed Turkish attacks. An Italian military engineer called Paolo Floriani was responsible for the defences, and so the suburb was named after him. Today, the most prominent features are the war memorials and the monuments to Maltese worthies.

Maglio Gardens

This tree-lined walk through central Floriana was once a recreational ground where the Knights were supposed to work off their excess energy and thereby distract themselves from ideas of more lustful pursuits. Among the monuments is a statue of Grand Master de Vilhena, which was taken from Republic Square (then known as Queen's Square) in Valletta to make way for a statue of Queen Victoria.

The large Independence Arena to the north, once the old military Parade Ground, is now used as a sports ground. To one end of the gardens, the Argotti Botanical Gardens have exotic plants, and some unusually rare species of cactus.

Between Il-Mall (The Mall) and Triq il-Sarria (Sarria St).

Porte des Bombes

Forming the entrance to Floriana, this ceremonial gateway was built between 1697 and 1720. In the 19th century the arch was doubled, and the curtain walls cut away to enable traffic to pass on either side.

Ħamrun

Ħamrun has some good shops, and is still known for basket-weaving. Otherwise the most interesting feature is the 17th-century aqueduct stretching between Ħamrun and Mdina. At Santa Venera, between Ħamrun and Birkirkara, the Casa Leone (*closed to the public*) was built in 1730 for Grand Master de Vilhena.

Qormi

Once known as Casal Fornaro (meaning the 'Village of Bakers'), Qormi still has a reputation for its bread, though the old baking methods are fast disappearing. The old quarter of narrow streets north of the town has some finely carved doorways and balconies. One of the earliest buildings is Stagno Palace (1589) in Dun Marigo Street, whose unusual façade has good examples of the typical Maltese 'fat' mouldings. The graceful Church of St George, at the eastern end of Qormi, was built at the end of the 16th century and still retains its Renaissance façade.

St Publius Church

This large, twin-towered church was named after the Roman governor of the island who was converted by St Paul. It was built in the 18th century, but has been remodelled and restored since. The circular slabs in St Publius Square cover the old underground granaries. Behind the church the Sarria Chapel has paintings by Mattia Preti.
Pjazza San Publiju (St Publius Square).
Open: for services on Sat evening & Sun morning. Free admission.

St Julian's

From a simple fishing village, St Julian's has grown into a busy resort, sought after for its restaurants, bars and nightlife. Spinola Bay, surrounded by waterside cafés and restaurants, retains its brightly painted fishing boats, although these days fishing activities are increasingly dwarfed by tourism. Evenings begin here with a drink or a meal (anything from a Chinese takeaway to French haute cuisine); then, as the night draws on, the general drift is towards the discos of Paceville.

Balluta Bay, on the Sliema side, lacks the colour of Spinola Bay, but has pleasant palm-lined gardens by the water's edge, and a water-polo pool where the local team (one of the best in Malta) excites the crowds on Saturday evenings in summer.

St Julian's most blatant concession to tourism is the Paceville area, north of St Julian's Bay, where video bars, pubs and fast-food outlets vie for space among blocks of hotels and apartments. Dominating the rocky shoreline is the Portomaso development, with a Hilton hotel, business tower, yacht marina and de-luxe residences. On Dragonara Point the casino occupies an elegant 19th-century mansion which belonged to Sir Hannibal Scicluna, founder of the first Maltese Bank.

On its north side Paceville merges with St Andrew's, once a large base for British military forces. The elegantly arcaded barracks are still in evidence.

Around the headland, St George's Bay has seen the rise of three large luxury hotels. The sandy beach, enlarged with sand imported from Jordan, is suitable for children, with shallow, sheltered waters.

Sliema

Set on a headland between Marsamxett Harbour and the open sea, Sliema is Malta's number-one tourist area. It is also the island's most densely populated town. A century ago this was a quiet area, with a few houses, the odd tower and a small chapel. Then wealthy Vallettans came and built their elegant Art Nouveau residences along the promenade. The introduction of the bus service in the 1920s accelerated development, and Sliema became a fashionable address. Today, it is the largest and the most expensive residential area in Malta.

With the rash of high-rise development now dwarfing what remains of old Sliema, the town could hardly be described as beautiful. Along Triq it-Torri (Tower Road) the few surviving old façades now look distinctly forlorn. In some cases there is literally no more than a façade, waiting to be demolished and replaced by a faceless modern flat or office block.

On the plus side, Sliema is a lively resort, with an excellent location and facilities. Valletta lies just across the water, and its dramatic skyline can be seen clearly from the Sliema Creek waterfront. The capital is easily reached by bus or ferry. Sliema is also the starting point for cruises, and is well placed for touring the island. All visitor destinations are within a 40-minute bus ride of the town.

There are no sandy beaches, but the coastline shelves gently to the water, and the smooth rocks and lidos on the north side afford good swimming. A 5km (3-mile) promenade runs all the way from Gżira, just southwest of Sliema, to St Julian's Bay, passing gardens and playgrounds.

On the south side of the headland, the Strand is the livelier of the two

VALLETTA–SLIEMA FERRIES

Sliema lies northwest of Valletta, across Marsamxett Harbour. Ferries to Valletta leave roughly every half-hour from near the junction of the Strand and Triq it-Torri. The quay at Valletta is very steep. Buses 60, 63, 68 and many others leave every few minutes.

promenades. Here you can watch cruisers steam across Sliema Creek, and ferries on their way to Valletta. A dual carriageway separates the promenade from a commercialised strip of souvenir shops, cafés and restaurants.

The shopping centre, where you can find everything from toasters to high fashion, lies between the two main promenades, where the road cuts across the headland. The Tigné Peninsula, jutting towards Valletta, has been blighted by the Tigné Point Development. This vast complex comprises some 450 residential units, a business centre, a piazza and Malta's largest shopping mall, The Point.

Gżira, the town that lies just southwest of Sliema, is primarily residential. A bridge links it to Manoel

Sliema

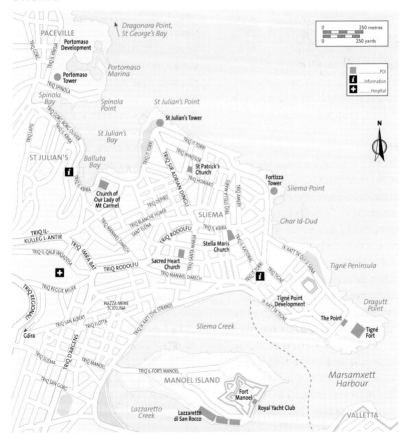

Fashionable St Julian's is the place to eat out or dance the night away

Island, home to the Royal Yacht Club. Fort Manoel and Lazzaretto di San Rocco (the former quarantine station) are both undergoing restoration as part of the Tigné Point Development. Low-rise apartment blocks, a five-star hotel, a heritage centre and shops are planned for the site.

THE THREE CITIES

When the Knights of St John acquired Malta they chose to settle in the area known as Il Borgo del Castello, which later became Birgù. The only alternative would have been to settle in Mdina, but this might have aroused the hostility of the Maltese nobility who were already deeply ensconced there. In any case, Birgù offered a safe anchorage for the Knights' galleys. Thus, they chose this long peninsula on which to build their first *auberges* and *palazzi*.

It was after the epic Siege of 1565 that Grand Master La Valette decided to give Birgù the new name of Vittoriosa (the Victorious). To the locals, however, it is still, and always will be, Birgù.

Vittoriosa is the most interesting of the so-called Three Cities – the other two being Senglea and Cospicua. The name 'cities' is somewhat misleading. The thin peninsula which forms Vittoriosa is only 1km (²/₃ mile) long, and the population is 3,200. It feels more like a small town than a city. Senglea is also spread out on a long, thin peninsula, separated from Vittoriosa by Dockyard Creek. Cospicua links the two, its stalwart ring of forts protecting the cities on the landward side.

GETTING TO THE THREE CITIES

The Three Cities lie across the Grand Harbour from Valletta. The quickest access is via a *dghajsa* (harbour water taxi) or there are regular buses from Valletta (for Cospicua, Nos 1, 2, 3, 4 & 6; for Senglea, No 3; for Vittoriosa, Nos 1, 2, 4 & 6).

Cospicua (formerly called Bormla) was renamed after its (conspicuous) role during the siege. Just to confuse things further, the city of Senglea was originally called L'Isla; it was renamed Senglea when it was fortified by Grand Master Claude de la Sèngle, but this was changed to Città Invicta (Unconquered City) after the Great Siege of 1565. Today, it is referred to as Senglea.

The dockyards in the area made an obvious target for German bombs during World War II. Most of Cospicua and Senglea was reduced to rubble, and the rebuilt suburbs are uninspiring. Saving graces are Cospicua's fortifications and Senglea's picturesque waterfront, while Vittoriosa has a charming centre. Northeast of the Three Cities at Kalkara, the 19th-century British-built Fort Rinella, with its 100-ton gun, is open to the public after undergoing extensive restoration.

The Cottonera Waterfront

The aim of the Cottonera Waterfront Regeneration Project was to transform the formerly abandoned quaysides of the Three Cities into a major cultural, commercial and recreational area for locals and tourists. Vittoriosa's waterfront has already undergone a transformation, with the swish new Grand Harbour Marina, luxury apartments and the Casino Venezia (complete with harbour-view restaurant) converted from the Captain-General's palace. The former dockyard has been converted into a bustling yachting marina. The old warehouses lining the waterfront now host a number of elegant restaurants, including Two and a Half Lemon and Malta's first vegetarian restaurant, the Tate, with tables laid out on the quayside. At the end of the Vittoriosa Waterfront in the Sea Gate Vaults under the majestic Fort St Angelo is the Lupanara wine bar and bistro.

Across Dockyard Creek the Senglea quayside is in line for restoration and, when complete, the

The Church of the Immaculate Conception in Cospicua

The impressive harbourfront at Senglea

waterfronts of Vittoriosa and Senglea will be integrated into one long promenade.

Senglea

The best thing today about Senglea is the view from the waterfront. A magnificent vantage point for Valletta and the Grand Harbour is the Safe Haven Garden, laid out in 1922. The original *vedette*, or lookout tower, with its symbolic sculptured eye and ear, still watches over the harbour.

The ornate Church of Our Lady of Victories, which was almost entirely destroyed in the war, has since been completely restored.

Vittoriosa (Birgù)

From 1530 until 1571 Birgù was home to the Knights. Of the Three Cities, it is the one that has altered the least. As the old capital, it has some imposing sites, including Fort St Angelo, the Church of St Lawrence, the Inquisitor's Palace and the *auberges* of the Knights.

You will find many tiny shops and beautiful ancient houses along its winding streets. The Maritime Museum, the Malta at War Museum and Vittoriosa 1565 are worth a visit.

Church of St Lawrence

The majestic Baroque Church of St Lawrence has a fine setting overlooking Dockyard Creek. Built in the 16th century, this was the Knights' conventual church until St John's Co-Cathedral was built in Valletta. The Maltese architect Lorenzo Gafà designed the church. Miraculously, the greater part of the church survived the bombing raids of World War II. Those parts that were damaged have been rebuilt, and the dome has been redesigned on a larger scale. Inside, the vault is decorated with paintings depicting episodes from the life of St Lawrence. The finest work of art is Mattia Preti's large altarpiece, *The Martyrdom of St Lawrence*. There is also a huge statue of the city's patron saint. Besides St Joseph's Oratory the small museum contains treasures brought by the Knights from Rhodes, including the sword of Grand Master Jean Parisot de la Valette. A statue in front of the

The Three Cities

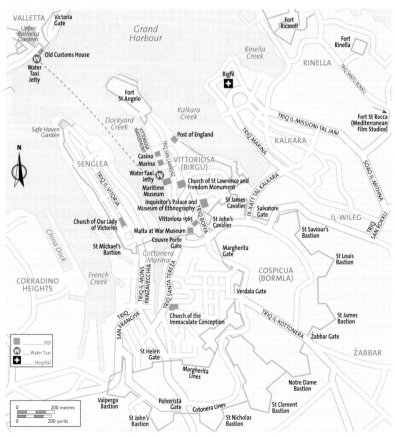

church depicting a British soldier shaking hands with a local docker commemorates the withdrawal of the British forces from Malta in 1979.
Triq San Lawrenz (St Lawrence St). Church open: Mon–Sat 6am–7pm. The museum has erratic opening times. Free admission but donation appreciated.

Fort St Angelo

On the tip of Vittoriosa, commanding the harbour, Fort St Angelo was the Knights' most impressive fortress. It is believed to have been the site of a Phoenician and, later, a Roman temple. It was fortified by the Arabs in the 9th century, then again by the Normans and the Aragonese in the 11th and 13th centuries. Between 1530 and 1576 it was the headquarters of the Order of St John, and during the Great Siege it bore the brunt of the Turkish attacks after the fall of St Elmo. After 1576 Fort St Angelo became the state prison of the Order.

More recently the fortress was garrisoned by the British armed forces. From 1903 to 1979 it was the headquarters of the Royal Navy. The exterior walls facing Valletta are often used for light shows, banners and fireworks during festivals and regattas. The interior of the fort is not open to the public but there are long-term plans eventually to develop it into a cultural attraction.
The fort is currently closed to the public.

Inquisitor's Palace

This palace is a grim reminder of the days of the Inquisition in Malta. Established in 1562 and abolished by the French in 1798, the Office of the Inquisition was set up to protect the Catholic faith and combat heresy. The official Inquisitor was a powerful figure who often abused his authority and became thoroughly unpopular with the Knights, with whom he was supposed to cooperate. The palace was used by the Inquisitors from 1574 as their residence, court and prison.

The palace was built in the 1530s and originally served as the civil law courts for the Order of St John. Today, it is home to the **Museum of Ethnography**, which focuses on Maltese religious culture and the impact of the Inquisition on Maltese society. Other areas open to the public are the Tribunal Room, the Main Hall (whose ceiling is decorated with the Inquisitors' coats of arms carved in wood) and the dungeons where you can still see graffiti scratched by the prisoners.
Triq il-Mina il-Kbira (Main Gate St). Tel: (356) 21827006. Open: daily 9am–5pm. Admission charge.

Malta at War Museum

The air-raid shelter under the Couvre Porte, the medieval entrance to Birgù, was converted into a museum at the end of 2002. It combines a permanent exhibition on World War II and the

shelter. The museum is housed in a 19th-century barracks built in the bastions. The shelter is a maze of tunnels which are more than 1km (⅔ mile) long and which could accommodate up to 500 people. The museum showcases an impressive collection of period memorabilia and illustrates how shelters were dug.
Couvre Porte. Tel: (356) 21896617.
Open: Tue–Sun 10am–5pm.
Guided tours on the hour with a showing of a wartime film.
Admission charge.

Maritime Museum

In 1842 the naval bakery was built over the site of the old slipway where the Knights repaired their galleys, and it remained a naval establishment until the British left Malta in 1979. It is now a maritime museum of Malta's remarkable seafaring heritage, with sections on the navy of the Knights, the Royal Navy, fishing vessels, the merchant navy and traditional Maltese boats.
The Waterfront. Tel: (356) 21660052.
Open: daily 9am–5pm.
Admission charge.

Post of England

This lookout point on the Kalkara Creek side of the Vittoriosa Peninsula affords fine views of the seaward end of the Grand Harbour.

Fort St Angelo protected Valletta and its harbour

64

Central Malta

Malta's central section, stretching from the Victoria Lines to the Valletta conurbation, is a region of gentle hills, terraced fields, farms and a number of ever-expanding villages and towns. The Victoria Lines, following the natural escarpment across the island, is a chain of British-built forts stretching from Madliena in the east to the great Bingemma Fort in the west. These were built to defend the most populated parts of the island from enemy landings in the west.

South of the Victoria Lines is Mdina, the jewel in Malta's crown, and a must for any visitor. The city's dynamic cathedral dome and the great walls of

Malta's former capital rise above the plains of central Malta and command a huge sweep of the Maltese landscape. Just outside Mdina is the suburb of

Mdina and Rabat

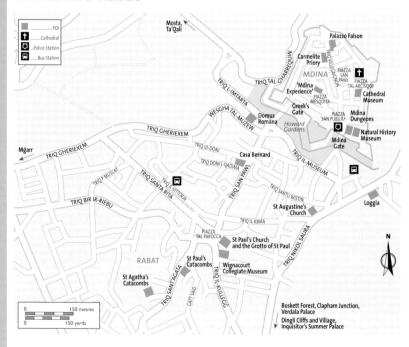

Rabat, best known for the labyrinth of catacombs beneath its streets. It is also a town of craftsmen, some of whom can be seen at work in the nearby village of Ta'Qali. Central Malta's other great cultural highlight is Mosta, whose colossal church dome is a conspicuous landmark from almost any vantage point in the area.

Although the region is essentially rocky and treeless, it contains two of the greenest spots on the island: Buskett Forest is the only place on the Maltese archipelago where trees grow in profusion; and the gardens of the San Anton Palace have some of the most exotic flower and plant species to be found on any of the islands.

MDINA

It is hard to believe that the earthquake of 1693 destroyed most of Mdina's

TRANSPORT TO CENTRAL MALTA

Mdina is 10km (6 miles) west of Valletta. Bus 65 from Sliema, buses 80, 81 & 84 from Valletta.

medieval and Sicilian-Norman buildings. Thanks to expert restoration, this gem of a town gives every impression of having survived the ravages of time.

Crowning a hilltop at the centre of Malta, the cathedral dome and the walls surrounding the city can be seen from far away. Justifiably, it is known as the Silent City. Today's population is a mere 400, and most inhabitants appear to stay behind the tightly closed doors of their handsome town houses. It is rare that you get the chance to see into one of the lovely inner courtyards.

Only city residents are allowed to bring cars through the city gates

Central Malta

The ancient citadel of Mdina is one of Malta's highlights

(commercial vehicles until 10.30am); for most of the day the streets are peaceful, and there is little sign of commerce. The only concessions to tourism are a handful of gift shops, a few inconspicuous restaurants, and one 17-room luxury hotel which occupies an old *palazzo*. The town is essentially one of peaceful alleys, handsome *palazzi*, old mansions and interesting museums. Nothing has been allowed to spoil its essentially medieval character. Even when large groups of tourists do descend on the city, it manages to retain a remarkably calm and dignified air.

Architecture

Mdina is one of the few great architectural treats on Malta that did not result from the activities of the Knights of St John. Originally built by

Mdina's architecture varies from medieval to more recent neo-Gothic

the Romans, the city was named Melita. Under the Arabs it was reduced to its present size, refortified, and given the name of Mdina, which means 'city' in Arabic. Rabat then became the suburb. Under Aragonese rule Mdina took on the medieval character that it preserves today, and it was Alfonso V of Aragon who named it Città Notabile (Eminent City). Once the Knights built Valletta as the new capital, Mdina lost its worthy name and became simply the Città Vecchia, or Old City.

Mdina has always been the home of noble families and dignitaries. A famous former resident was Malta's first bishop, Publius, who was converted to Christianity by St Paul; Malta's oldest titled family still resides in one of the palaces. Many of the residences were left empty for long periods when their owners moved to Valletta to join the Knights, but now almost all the old houses are lovingly maintained, and any in disrepair are rapidly being restored.

The streets are narrow and winding, flanked by the mellow golden façades of Baroque and restored medieval mansions. Many of them have fine stone or wrought-iron balconies, and elaborate brass knockers on the doors. Despite the disparity in age between the medieval and the later Baroque, the architecture, as a whole, is extraordinarily harmonious.

Most of the finest dwellings front on to Triq Villegaignon (Villegaignon St), the city's major thoroughfare, which

The conspicuous dome of Mdina's cathedral rises to dizzying heights

leads in a more or less straight line to the fortified northern edge of the city. From here there are wonderful views across the plains to Valletta. The alleys leading off Villegaignon Street were deliberately built narrow and angled to deflect the flight of arrows and shot. These silent alleys, off the beaten tourist track, are well worth exploring.

Carmelite Priory

This is a restored 17th-century priory now open as a museum. The friars' dining room (refectory) is an extraordinary example of Baroque art and design. Concerts are held on Saturdays and the church has an impressive painting of *The Annunciation* above the main altar. The Old Priory Café serves lunch and afternoon tea.

Triq Villegaignon (Villegaignon St). Tel: (356) 27020404.

www.carmelitepriorymuseum.com. Open: daily 10am–5pm. Admission charge.

The cathedral

The devastating earthquake of 1693 almost totally destroyed Mdina's old cathedral. The original church dated back to the 13th century, and can be seen in two of Matteo Perez d'Aleccio's frescoes in the Grand Master's Palace in Valletta. Less than ten years after its collapse, a new Baroque church had risen in its place.

The cathedral was designed by the well-known Maltese architect Lorenzo Gafà. By this time he had already designed several churches on Malta, and was at the height of his career. The perfectly proportioned façade and the dynamic dome (by far his boldest and arguably the finest on Malta) make this the most impressive of all his churches.

Sturdy balconies and Baroque enrichments abound in the streets around the cathedral

The work took just five years to complete, and a number of houses were demolished at the same time to make way for a piazza appropriate to the size and splendour of the church.

Inside, the immediate impression is one of grandeur. Although not quite as rich as St John's Co-Cathedral in Valletta, it is nevertheless reminiscent of that church in the gilded carvings, the ornamental side chapels, and the paintings that adorn the vault, apse and chapels. Many of the paintings and carvings illustrate scenes from the life of St Paul; the finest (but not the easiest to see) is Mattia Preti's mural of *The Shipwreck of St Paul*, decorating the apse. This was one of the few treasures in the old church which survived the earthquake.

As in Valletta's cathedral, the floor is inlaid with funerary slabs in multi-coloured marble commemorating bishops, prelates and various members of the Maltese aristocracy.
*Pjazza San Pawl (St Paul's Square).
Open: Mon–Sat 9am–1pm &
1.30–4.30pm. Admission charge jointly
with Cathedral Museum.*

Cathedral Museum

Treasures salvaged from the original pre-earthquake cathedral are now housed in a splendid Baroque palace which once served as a Diocesan seminary. The collection of paintings, prints, woodcuts and Old Master drawings is the legacy of Count Saverio Marchese (1757–1833), a wealthy patron of the arts. Particularly fine among the works of art are the woodcuts by Dürer, the engravings by Rembrandt, and the 14th-century St Paul Polyptych, which once adorned the high altar of the old cathedral.

Among the other museum exhibits are finely illustrated choir books, elaborate vestments, silver plates and a coin collection spanning over 2,000 years. The old refectory of the seminary has been preserved, as has the 18th-century octagonal chapel.

Pjazza Tal-Arċisqof (Archbishop's Square). Tel: (356) 21454697. Open: Mon–Fri 9.30am–4.45pm, Sat 9.30am–3.30pm. Closed: Sun & public holidays. Admission charge.

Mdina Dungeons

The chambers, cells and secret underground passageways below the Palazzo Vilhena (Vilhena Palace) form the setting for Malta's most gruesome museum. Here, the darker side of Malta's history is presented in a series of horrific waxwork scenes. Be prepared for gory scenes of torture and execution, dead rats, death-carts, heads on spikes, and harlots and witches being whipped. Such scenes are a reminder that torture was only publicly and formally abolished in 1813 by Sir Thomas Maitland, British Governor of Malta.

Pjazza San Publiju (St Publius Square). Tel: (356) 21450267. Open: daily 9.30am–4pm. Admission charge.

'Mdina Experience'

This audiovisual show, in 12 languages, takes you through the tragedies and triumphs of the old capital. The auditorium occupies part of a well-converted 'Norman' house, which can

also be admired while you take a drink at the bar.

7 Pjazza Mesquita (Mesquita Square). Tel: (356) 21450055. Open: daily 10am–4.30pm. Hourly shows. Admission charge.

Natural History Museum

The magisterial Palazzo Vilhena is French in style, and one of its finest features is the sculpted doorway, showing the coat of arms of Grand Master Manoel de Vilhena, who built it in the 18th century. The palace was later used as a temporary hospital during the outbreak of cholera in 1837,

Old mansions line the narrow streets of Mdina

then as a military hospital for British troops from 1860.

Today, the palace makes a fine setting for the Natural History Museum. This is a pleasantly old-fashioned museum, with spacious rooms and excellent labelling in English. Different sections are devoted exclusively to minerals, fossils, fish, insects, mammals and birds.
Pjazza San Publiju (St Publius Square). Tel: (356) 21455951. Open: daily 9am–5pm. Admission charge.

Palazzo Falson

The so-called Norman House was built in 1495 ('Norman' in Malta means

anything from 1090, when the Normans arrived, to 1530, when the island was handed over to the Knights). This finely preserved mansion, with its graceful arched windows, has been lovingly restored. The last owner was Captain Olof Frederick Gollcher (1889–1962), an artist, scholar and philanthropist, and a discerning collector of art and antiques. Silver, jewellery, paintings and curious *objets d'art* are displayed within small, intimate rooms. An added attraction is the rooftop café commanding sweeping views of Malta.
Triq Villegaignon (Villegaignon St). Tel: (356) 21454512. Email: info@palazzofalson.com. www.palazzofalson.com. Open: Tue–Sun 10am–5pm (8pm on Sat & Sun in summer). Last admission one hour before closing time. Admission charge.

RABAT

Compared with the little medieval city of Mdina, silently enclosed within its walls, Rabat is sprawling, bustling and very much alive. This is, after all, the commercial hub of central Malta. Unlike Mdina, Rabat has plenty of bars, shops and local life.

In Roman times Rabat and Mdina were one city. It was the Arabs who dug a ditch to isolate and protect Mdina, making Rabat the suburb. Today, the town is visited for its churches, chapels, Roman remains and catacombs (*see map on p64*).

The Grotto of St Paul, either the church or prison of the saint

St Paul's Church is built on the spot where the saint is said to have once preached

Casa Bernard

This 16th-century historic mansion is the home of a Maltese noble family, and one of them will show you round. *46 Triq San Pawl (St Paul's St). Tel: (356) 21451888. www.casabernard.com. Open for tours: Mon–Sat 10am, 11am, noon & 1pm or by appointment. Admission charge.*

Catacombs

The whole area beneath Rabat is honeycombed with catacombs – underground burial chambers. They date back to the period between the 3rd and 7th centuries AD, when people dug tombs, canopies and tables out of the soft rock. Over 3sq km (1sq mile) of chambers have been discovered. Some can be visited by the public.

St Agatha's Catacombs

The small church of St Agatha is dedicated to a young Sicilian saint who, according to local tradition, crossed to Malta to escape persecution during the reign of Emperor Decius (3rd century AD). The church's crypt is decorated with a fascinating series of Gothic and Renaissance frescoes, depicting St Agatha and other saints. St Agatha's Catacombs lie below the church: there are pagan, Punic and Jewish burial chambers within this catacomb complex, but only the Christian section is open to the public.

The dark, narrow passageways are flanked by tombs of small groups or families, often with a circular stone table, known as an agape table. It was here that ritualised funeral feasts took place to celebrate the anniversary of the death of relatives or friends. These tables were later replaced by altars. Remnants of ancient frescoes are just visible on a few of the tomb walls.

In the convent next to the church is a museum that has some interesting displays of ancient pottery and prehistoric animal remains, including a mummified alligator (600–400 BC).
Off Triq Sant'Agata (St Agatha's St). Tel: (356) 21454503. Open: Mon–Fri 9am–4.30pm, Sat 9am–12.30pm. Guided tours only. Admission charge.

St Paul's Catacombs

The largest of Rabat's catacomb complexes, this is an extraordinary labyrinth of narrow passages lined by rock-cut tombs. Like the catacombs of St Agatha, some of these have an agape table hewn out of the rock.
Triq Sant'Agata (St Agatha's St). Tel: (356) 21454562. Open: daily 9am–5pm. Admission charge.

Domus Romana

Although called the Domus Romana (Roman House), it is actually housed in a 1920s neoclassical building, albeit on the site of a Roman town house whose original mosaic floor is an important exhibit. Other examples of mosaic work decorate the walks along with columns,

capitals, statues and tombstones which have been unearthed in the area. Among the other finds are early Christian oil lamps, Roman glass, Punic amphorae and ancient bronze fish-hooks.
Wesgha Tal-Mużew (Museum Esplanade). Tel: (356) 21454125. Open: summer daily 9am–5pm. Admission charge.

St Paul's Church and the Grotto of St Paul

The parish church of Rabat, founded in 1575, but remodelled in 1692, was built over one of Malta's earliest Christian chapels. The Grotto of St Paul, below the adjoining Chapel of St Publius, is the main point of interest. According to the locals, it was here that St Paul spent several weeks preaching Christianity; another story has it that the Apostle was imprisoned here.

It is also said that stone scraped from the grotto walls has special healing powers and that, however much stone

CART RUTS

The tracks that criss-cross several rocky plateaux on Malta and Gozo have been a puzzle to archaeologists. Sometimes called 'the tramlines of Neolithic man', they cut across the limestone in parallel lines, usually 1.35m (4½ft) apart. There are various theories as to their purpose, but it is generally agreed they were made by, or created for, some sort of transport system. They may have been formed by the constant use of animal-drawn sledges, or they may have been carved to guide a wheeled vehicle. Neither theory explains why some of the cart ruts, such as those at Clapham Junction, lead off the edge of the cliffs.

is scraped away, the cave never alters in size. The prominent feature, below a series of dimly lit catacombs, is a marble statue of St Paul.

The custodian will inform you that the grotto was once a Roman prison, and will show you the holes in the roof from where the prisoners' chains once hung. Two tiny chapels are dedicated to St Paul and St Luke, each one with a statue of its Apostle.

St Paul's Grotto, Pjazza Tal-Parocca (Parish Square). Tel: (356) 21454467. Open: daily 9.30am–1.30pm & 2.30–5pm. No admission charge, but a tip to the custodian is welcomed. Entrance in the main square.

Wignacourt Collegiate Museum

This former clergy house is linked to St Paul's Church by an underground passage. In 1981 the college was converted to a museum and picture gallery where you can see Punic-Roman pottery, old maps, coins, books and furniture.

Triq il-Kulleġġ (College St), by St Paul's Church. Tel: (356) 21451060. Open: Mon–Sat 10am–2.30pm. Admission charge.

RABAT ENVIRONS
Buskett Forest

In summer Buskett Forest is a green oasis. The name is a corruption of the Italian *boschetto*, meaning 'small wood'. The paths are lined by pines and firs, cypresses and oaks, citrus and mulberry trees.

The forest is green all year, although more rewarding in spring than in summer. The area is a public park, popular with both locals and visitors, especially at the end of June when it becomes the venue of the *Imnarja* festival.

A focal point of the forest is the long-established Buskett Roadhouse, where you can try Maltese cuisine, and dance on summer evenings.

4km (2½ miles) south of Rabat. Free admission. Bus 81, Valletta to Dingli.

Clapham Junction

Clapham Junction is the name for the site of numerous prehistoric cart ruts – although to the uninitiated eye they are not immediately obvious. Look for the intersecting grooves carved into the limestone, and running towards the cliffs (*see box opposite*).

Għajn il-Kbira (0.5km/⅓ mile from Buskett Forest). Free admission.

Verdala Palace, overlooking Buskett Forest

Terraces tumble down the hillside in the area around Dingli Cliffs

Dingli Cliffs

The highest village on Malta, Dingli lies on the west side of the island where the cliffs drop 253m (830ft) to the sea. For those with a head for heights this remote and dramatic stretch of coast makes wonderful walking territory, particularly in spring when tiny wild irises sprout from seemingly solid rock. Five kilometres (3 miles) offshore, the steep rocky islet of Filfla rises up from the blue sea.

From the road skirting the cliff tops, the first impression you gain of the coastline is of a sheer drop to the sea. A glance over the cliff tops reveals, at least 100m (330ft) below, a wide shelf of neatly terraced and surprisingly fertile fields. Not so many years ago fishermen used to lower themselves from the terraces by knotted rope, clinging to the rope with one hand, and precariously casting out a line with the

other. The lonely Magdalena Chapel perches on the coastline's highest point. This opens just once a year, for the feast of St Magdalene on 22 July. An inscription warns that the chapel cannot offer sanctuary from the law – a legacy of the 17th century, when the Order of St John restricted the refuge offered by the church.

The only other real landmarks are a radar station and, along the aptly named Panoramic Road, a restaurant called Bobbyland, which can provide a good rabbit stew and breathtaking views from the terrace.

Dingli Village

The village of Dingli lies just over 1km (²/₃ mile) inland from the cliffs, the silver dome of its church dominating the skyline. The road runs through a stony landscape irrigated by water drawn up from below ground by slim

metal wind-driven pumps. Dingli is an unassuming village with a cluster of houses around the church and a handful of welcoming bars and cafés.
3km (1³/4 miles) southwest of Rabat. Bus 81 from Valletta.

Inquisitor's Summer Palace

This was built in 1625, and the caves below it were used as staff quarters – or so the story goes. For years it was abandoned and lay victim to vandals. Now it is the official summer residence of the prime minister. Guards will ensure you get no further than the gates of the palace. The Inquisitors chose well, for it lies in the beautiful Girgenti Valley, which is full of fragrant citrus groves.
Not open to the public.

Verdala Palace

It is perhaps not surprising that Grand Master Hughes Loubenx de Verdalle, who was renowned for his love of pomp and splendour, chose one of the finest settings on the island for his summer retreat. The palace overlooks the woods and citrus groves of the Buskett Forest (*see p73*).

The building was designed by Gerolamo Cassar in 1586 on the lines of a fortified castle. The moat surrounding the palace saw several suicides during de Verdalle's reign. The Grand Master was notoriously cruel, and, to some of his servants, drowning seemed preferable to the agonies of the torture chamber. French officers, imprisoned in the palace in 1812, left their mark in the game boards chiselled into the stone floor of the upstairs dining room. Today, the palace is one of the president's residences, and a showplace where VIPs are entertained.
2.5km (1¹/2 miles) south of Rabat. Not open to the public, except for special events.

The elegant Verdala Palace was built as a cool and shady summer retreat for the Grand Masters

Central Malta

Wine tourism

The climate in Malta and Gozo is ideal for grapes and wine production can be traced back to Roman times. However, it was only in the 1970s that Maltese wine production really took off as an industry with the introduction of vines cultivated successfully in France and Italy.

As prestige tourism grew and visitors demanded high-quality wines, Maltese producers upped their game to compete with high-quality imports. Now Maltese wines win awards alongside more established products from around Europe.

Maltese wine production is of course on a much smaller scale than in France, Italy or Spain, but it is celebrated in wine festivals around the time of harvesting the grapes, and with organised tours and tastings at the wineries and estates.

Juicy white grapes growing in a Gozo vineyard

Marsovin (*tel: (356) 23662260; www.marsovin.com*) is a household name in Malta. The company has been producing high-quality wine for over 100 years and has five vine-growing estates producing grapes for single estate premium wines. A tour of Marsovin's winery in Marsa lasts about two hours and takes place on Tuesdays and Thursdays; pre-booking is essential. The tour begins with a historical introduction, followed by a walk through some 400-year-old cellars. The wine-tasting session is an opportunity to sample the range of Marsovin wines under the guidance of highly trained staff. Marsovin promotes its wines in annual wine festivals in Valletta and Gozo in July.

Emmanuel Delicata (tel: (356) 2182 5199; www.delicata.com) is Malta's oldest family-run winemaker, established in 1907. The company sponsors wine festivals each year in August in the Upper Barracca Gardens in Valletta, and in Nadur, the grape-growing heart of Gozo, in September. The festivals coincide with the start and finish of the Maltese grape harvest. At least 20 wines are available to taste along with delicious local food. The Delicata winery is located on the waterfront at Paola. The cellars incorporate the company's tasting vaults and are used for wine-related educational training sessions. Tours by appointment.

Meridiana (tel: (356) 21413550; www.meridiana.com.mt) is a relatively young wine producer, founded in 1987. The Meridiana wine estate is in the countryside near the Ta'Qali Craft Centre below the walled city of Mdina. The vineyard is planted with Cabernet Sauvignon, Merlot, Syrah and Petit Verdot grape varieties. The wine cellars here are dug 4m (13ft) below ground level where the temperature is maintained naturally at about 20°C (68°F). Tours and wine tastings can be arranged. A selection of wines and merchandise is available at the Cellar Shop (open: Mon–Fri 9am–4pm, Sat 10am–noon).

Camilleri Wines (tel: (356) 25492000; www.camilleriwines.com) started in 2000 and launched their first Maltese-grown Chardonnay in 2004. Next to the winery in Naxxar is Master Cellars, a retail store with a custom-made tasting area.

Montekristo Estates (tel: (356) 21231448; www.montekristo.com) is one of the newest wineries in Malta, located near the village of Siġġiewi. The vineyard covers about 8 hectares (20 acres) and has a well-equipped modern winery. An estate shop sells wine, olive oil and other fine food items. The vast underground wine vaults storing oak barrels in rock-hewn chambers provide an original and highly impressive backdrop for wine tastings.

On a much smaller scale, wine is made at the **Ta'Mena Estate** on Gozo (tel: (356) 21555699; www.tamena-gozo.com), in an agritourism complex. They grow their own grapes and produce great wines with a particular Gozitan character, fruity and full-bodied. The estate is situated in the picturesque Marsalforn Valley and includes a fruit garden, olive and orange groves, and over 10 hectares (25 acres) of vineyards. As well as guided tours, cooking sessions followed by lunch or dinner are on offer.

Enjoying the pond and greenery in the gardens of San Anton Palace

THE THREE VILLAGES

The villages of Attard, Balzan and Lija have for many years been prosperous residential areas, typified by elegant residences and well-watered gardens, often hidden behind high walls. During the era of the Knights many affluent families moved away from crowded Valletta and set up their homes here. The villages have more or less merged into one, and only the locals seem to know where the divisions lie.

Attard

Church of St Mary

Attard's parish church is a remarkable achievement, built by Tommaso Dingli when he was only 22 years old. It was completed in 1613, and is one of the few noteworthy Renaissance buildings on Malta. The façade, reminiscent of a Roman temple, has a particularly fine carved doorway.

San Anton Palace

The French Grand Master Antoine de Paule (who took office in 1623) was notoriously vain and self-indulgent. The days of frugality within the Order were over, decadence had set in and de Paule was determined to lead a life of luxury. Considering Verdala Palace too far from Valletta for his comfort, he chose instead to enlarge this country house near the village of Attard, turning it into the sumptuous San Anton Palace. Here de Paule lived in great state along with his retinue of staff, including falconers, wig-makers, chefs, valets, domestic servants and a rat-catcher. To celebrate his first night in the palace, he gave a massive banquet and invited all his staff and numerous VIPs.

In later years Samuel Taylor Coleridge stayed at the beautiful palace and wrote of it, 'If living in lofty and splendid rooms be a pleasure, I have it.' In more recent history the luxurious palace served as residence of the British governors. Today, it is the private residence of the president.

The palace is not open to the public, but the gardens are.

San Anton Gardens

These luxuriant public gardens are laid out with avenues of trees, exotic shrubs and flowers. Apart from the cats that roam the gardens (many of them, sadly, abandoned by their owners), there is also a tiny zoo.

Gardens open daily till sunset. Free admission.

Balzan and Lija

Desirable villas and a variety of churches are the notable features of these two villages. In Balzan the

A Palm Sunday cross decorates one of Gudja's older buildings

late 17th-century **Church of the Annunciation** in the main square has a Baroque façade, and more than a hint of Spanish influence in its design. The simple little **Church of St Roch** in Three Churches Street was built in 1593, and dedicated to the protector of unfortunate victims of plague.

In Lija the handsome **Church of St Saviour** was built in 1694 by Giovanni Barbara. The essentially sober façade gives little hint of the elaborate frescoed interior. Lija has one of the island's most spectacular firework displays, held on the first Sunday after 6 August, and celebrating the Feast of St Saviour.

Gudja

Since the construction of Malta International Airport, this small farming village may have lost its identity, but it has managed to preserve a handful of its 17th- and 18th-century houses and four churches.

The small **Church of St Mary Ta'Bir Miftuh**, on the outskirts, is one of the oldest remaining churches on Malta, dating back to 1436. Gudja's principal claim to fame is that it was the birthplace of the great Maltese architect Gerolamo Cassar.

7km (4 miles) south of Valletta. Bus 8 from Valletta.

TRANSPORT FROM VALLETTA

The Three Villages lie about 6km (4 miles) west of Valletta. Bus 40 from Valletta to Attard, Balzan and Lija.

Mosta

To most people the village of Mosta means the church of Mosta or, more precisely, the massive dome. At the time of its completion in 1863 this was one of the few church domes in Europe that came close to the biggest of them all, St Peter's in Rome. No internal supports were used in its construction – it was only with the help of mules and pulleys that the huge slabs were hauled up. The edifice was built around an older, much smaller church, where services were held while construction work was in progress. The church, which can hold around 10,000 people, took 27 years to build, and, once it was completed, the old church was demolished.

The massive dome, which is totally out of proportion to the surrounding village, is visible from almost every vantage point in Malta. With its huge Ionic columns supporting the portico, the façade imitates the Pantheon in Rome.

The most compelling exhibit in the museum is a replica of the World War II bomb which penetrated the dome, fell among the congregation and, as if by a miracle, failed to explode. Photographs show the hole that the bomb ripped in the roof.

Mosta has two fine restaurants. The Lord Nelson is in a converted town house and a table on the typical Maltese balcony will give a wonderful view of the rotunda. Ta'Marija is renowned as one of the best

Mosta's church dominates the village

The monumental church of Mosta is crowned by one of Europe's biggest domes

places to find authentic Maltese cuisine and has won many awards.
8.5km (5¹/₄ miles) west of Valletta. Tel: (356) 21433826. Open: Mon–Sat 9am–noon & 3–5pm. Buses 49, 58 & others from Valletta.

Naxxar

Said to be one of the first villages to convert to Christianity after St Paul's arrival on the island, Naxxar is also one of the oldest villages in Malta. According to legend, St Paul preached in the chapel of San Pawl tat-Tarġa, just north of Naxxar. This small village is also known for its prehistoric cart tracks *(see p72)*.

Nowadays, Naxxar merges with Mosta and is best known as the venue of the Malta International Trade Fair *(1–15 July)*. The **Palazzo Parisio**, which was lavishly redeveloped in the 19th century, has the most ornate ballroom on Malta and the finest gardens on the islands.
8.5km (5¹/₄ miles) northwest of Valletta. Palazzo Parisio tel: (356) 21412461. www.palazzoparisio.com. Open: Mon–Fri 9am–4pm. Guided tours on the hour. Admission charge. Bus 55 from Valletta.

Siġġiewi

The predominant feature of this large farming village is the Baroque church

Making Maltese crosses of polished marble in Ta'Qali Craft Centre

of St Nicholas, and its crowning glory is its magnificent dome – one of the tallest in Malta. The church was designed by Lorenzo Gafà in 1675, though part of the exterior is a 19th-century addition. The huge piazza outside the church is best seen on a Sunday morning, when you can mingle with the local people, all dressed in their Sunday best.
6km (3¾ miles) southeast of Rabat. Bus 89 from Valletta.

Ta'Qali Craft Centre

The former World War II aerodrome at Ta'Qali is now the venue for the island's largest craft market. Although clearly aimed at the tourist market (it is one of the main stops on organised tours of the island), the prices here tend to be slightly cheaper than souvenir shops in resorts and towns. The wartime Nissen huts of the airbase make uninspiring showrooms, but at least you can see all the Maltese handicrafts in one complex, and you can watch the artisans at work: silversmiths fashioning filigree, metal workers beating brass and iron, lacemakers creating delicate shawls and tableware. The glass factory, on a limb from the rest of the complex, is perhaps the most impressive of the outlets, with a lovely range of vivid turquoise vases, glasses and decorative items. You can see the furnaces and watch the glass being blown before browsing in the air-conditioned shop. Prices are not high, especially if you choose from the range of 'seconds'. Ta'Qali also has an Aviation Museum.

For the Maltese, Ta'Qali's main draw is the national football stadium – venue for many international matches.
3.5km (2¼ miles) northeast of Rabat,

well marked off the main Attard/Mdina road. Open: Mon–Fri 8am–4.30pm, Sat 8am–12.30pm. Free admission. Bus 65 goes direct from Sliema, buses 80 & 81 from Valletta, bus 86 from Buġibba.

Victoria Lines

Malta's great geological rift runs in a northeasterly direction from Ras ir-Raħeb, on the west coast, almost as far as Baħar iċ-Ċagħaq, on the east side of the island. This provided a natural defence for the British at the end of the 19th century. A line of detached forts, with supporting bastions, was constructed along the ridge, cutting off the shallow bays of the west, which potentially provided easy landing for invaders.

Parts of the forts and bastions making up the lines can still be seen – travelling either by car along minor roads, or along footpaths which command some magnificent views. Fort Mosta, built in 1878–85, is the only fort along the Victoria Lines still used by the army – these days the Maltese military.

Fort Madliena, built in 1878–80, stands 132m (433ft) above the sea, and commands clear views of the landing beaches at Salina, St Paul's Bay and Mellieħa. This setting made it an ideal location for the island's main radar station in World War II.

Wignacourt Aqueduct

When Alof de Wignacourt took on the role of Grand Master in 1601, his biggest headache was the desperate water shortage in Valletta. Water being plentiful around Mdina, he decided on the construction of an aqueduct stretching for 15km (9 miles) from the old city to the heart of Valletta. Stretches of this very impressive (but now disused) aqueduct can still be seen on the road from Valletta to Mdina.

Żebbuġ

The name Żebbuġ means 'olives', and at one time the olive groves around here were prolific. Today, Żebbuġ is approached by the De Rohan Arch, named after the penultimate Grand Master of the Knights of St John, Emmanuel de Rohan-Polduc (1775–97).

The town has several churches, the finest of which is St Philip, built in 1632 to accommodate the expanding parish and show off its wealth. It is thought to have been designed by Vittorio Cassar, son of Gerolamo. *4.5km (2¾ miles) southeast of Rabat. Bus 88 from Valletta.*

Sections of the impressive Wignacourt Aqueduct still stand on the Valletta–Mdina road

Walk: Mdina

The walk is a very short one, but at almost every step there is some fine mansion or architectural detail to admire. The route concentrates on the main street running through the town, but feel free to explore the narrow alleys off it. Mdina is so small you cannot get lost.

Allow 30 minutes.

Start at the Mdina Gate, the main entrance to the city.

1 Mdina Gate

The triumphal gate was built in 1724 by Grand Master de Vilhena to replace a drawbridge gate, the outline of which can still be seen. The moat below was first dug by the Arabs in the 9th century. Orange trees now thrive here, and part of the ditch is given over to handball and tennis courts. On the far side of Mdina Gate, look back to see the carved reliefs of the three patron saints of Malta: St Publius, St Paul and St Agatha.
Walk through the gate to the first square.

2 Pjazza San Publiju (St Publius' Square)

The Baroque Palazzo Vilhena (Vilhena Palace) on your right houses the Natural History Museum. On the left, the stocky Torre dello Stendardo was once lit with fires to warn of landings by enemy troops. Today, it is the police station.
Turn left, then right into the main street.

3 Triq Villegaignon (Villegaignon Street)

This main thoroughfare has many fine *palazzi*. Look out for architectural details, such as window mouldings, shrines, reliefs and door-knockers.
A short way up on the left, stop at the house with the huge Renaissance door-knocker with swinging nudes.

4 Casa Inguanez

This historic house is the home of Malta's oldest aristocratic family – the current baron's ancestors joined the upper echelons in 1350.
Walk on to the cathedral square.

5 Pjazza San Pawl (St Paul's Square)

The monumental twin-belfried cathedral dominates the square. Legend has it that this was the site of the house where St Paul converted Publius, governor of the island, to Christianity in AD 60.
Continue along Triq Villegaignon, passing the very old Palazzo Santa

Sophia on the left, the little Church of
St Roque on the right and, further up,
the Carmelite Priory with its distinctive
belfry. Opposite, Palazzo Constanzo
houses a restaurant and the 'Medieval
Times' exhibition. Beyond is the Palazzo
Falson (see p70).

6 Pjazza Tas-Sur (Bastion Square)

The square is a great place to admire
the magnificent panorama over half the
island. You can see Valletta in the
distance, and on exceptionally clear
days you can even spot Mount Etna on
the island of Sicily.

*Follow the ramparts to the right
until you reach a sign saying
'Tea Gardens'.*

7 Fontanella Café

This charming café occupies the
garden of an old *palazzo*, with
glorious views.

*Continue along the ramparts, then a
right and left turn will bring you back to
St Paul's Square. Walk past the cathedral
into Pjazza tal-Arċisqof (Archbishop's
Square), and follow Triq San Pawl (St
Paul's St) to the small square at its end.*

8 Xara Palace

For centuries the home of the Xara
family, this fine old mansion served
as an officers' mess in World War II.
Today, it is a luxury hotel.

*A right and left turn will bring you back
to your starting point.*

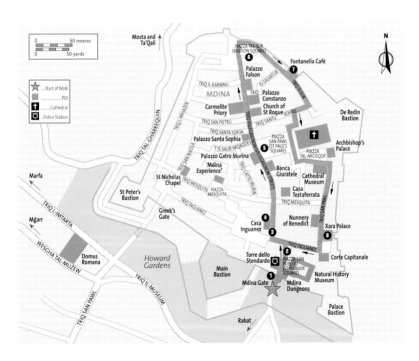

Café life

Like all Mediterranean countries, Malta has plenty of cafés, catering for both locals and tourists. The typical Maltese café is a friendly and relaxed place, where you can stop for a quick drink, or linger over a leisurely meal. The Maltese are a sweet-toothed nation, and most cafés have a range of pastries, cakes, biscuits and other tempting snacks.

The tourist boom inevitably produced a wealth of American-style fast food, but many cafés, especially in Valletta and inland towns, have Maltese specialities. Particularly popular are the *pastizzi rikotta* – small triangles of flaky puff pastry filled with ricotta and served hot. These are translated as 'cheesecakes', but are nothing like the American dessert. Other popular snacks among the locals are *hobz biz-zejt* (bread with oil, served with tomatoes, capers, tuna or other variations) and *mqaret* (date-filled pastries flavoured with aniseed and served deep-fried).

Every café will serve tea (a legacy of British rule), as well as coffee, and prices are very reasonable by European standards. Unlike most

Open-air cafés take full advantage of the weather

The cuisine is usually varied, though Maltese specialities, particularly seafood, are very popular

continental cafés, there is no price difference between standing at the bar for your drink or snack, or sitting at a table inside or on the terrace. Popular brands of soft drinks are available, as well as delicious fresh-fruit juices. *Kinnie*, a bitter-sweet aromatic drink made from herbs and bitter oranges, is something of an acquired taste. The British have also bequeathed to the Maltese a pale, fizzy ale sold almost everywhere under the Hopleaf and Cisk brands.

Two of the most inviting cafés in Malta are the Caffè Cordina in Republic Street, Valletta, which serves excellent cappuccino in elegant surroundings or on the square, and The Fontanella in Mdina, which has a magnificent panorama of the island.

Seaside cafés spring into life as soon as the tourists arrive in the spring, and for several months the warm weather ensures a roaring trade in ice creams, Maltese lagers and soft drinks.

Southern Malta

Southern Malta stretches from Żabbar to Żurrieq. The region's coastline is characterised by numerous bays, inlets and creeks. It is an area of caves and grottoes, temples and towers, and of pretty bays as well as ugly ones – recent changes have created a few eyesores. The seemingly endless conurbation stretching south and southeast of Valletta eventually gives way to agricultural land. Even here the villages are developing suburban tentacles that stretch further and further into the rural landscape.

For the visitor it is the coast that holds the attractions. Marsaxlokk, where traditional boats bob up and down on the intensely blue sea, is the prettiest of Malta's fishing villages. The fishing community still thrives here, and the village manages to cope with the daily influx of summer visitors without yielding to the trappings of tourism.

Southwest of the village, the only decent beach in Marsaxlokk Bay is spoilt by the proximity of Malta Freeport and the electricity-generating plant.

In the south, where dried-up river valleys drop down to coastal cliffs, the star attraction is the Blue Grotto below Wied iż-Żurrieq.

To the southeast, the region is rich in prehistoric sites. Għar Dalam, near Birżebbuġa, is a fascinating cave where the fossils of long-extinct animals were discovered. Sadly, the famous ancient sites of the Tarxien temples (*see pp106–7*) and the Ħal Saflieni Hypogeum (*see pp101–3*) are engulfed

by suburbia; in contrast, the ancient relics of Ħaġar Qim and Mnajdra sit silently and mysteriously above the sea, enclosed by protective canopies.

The Blue Grotto

Given good weather, calm seas and an honest boatman (many charge more than they should), a boat trip along the dramatic cliffs of the south coast is one of the highlights of a visit to Malta. To see the grottoes at their best, try to make the trip on a bright morning, preferably before 11am when the sun is still low enough for the rays to penetrate the deep caves.

The local fishermen ferry passengers from Wied iż-Żurrieq, a little fishing village on the south coast, reached by a spectacular drive along the cliffs. The traditional fishing boats run every day, provided that the waters are calm. In stormy weather the raging sea breaks on the headlands, sending spray high into the air. This alone makes driving to the southern coast worth the trip.

The village of Wied iż-Żurrieq consists of no more than a cluster of houses, shops and cafés, an exhibition of sea shells, a small shrine giving heavenly protection to fishermen, and a watchtower erected by the Knights to warn of enemy ships sighted on the horizon.

A slipway lined with fishing boats leads down to the minuscule harbour. This is a popular spot for swimmers and scuba divers. Fishermen cram in as many visitors as they can (eight is supposedly the limit), then set off for the 25-minute trip along the coast. The boats skirt weird-shaped cliffs, and weave in and out of a series of caverns, each one with a different name. On a fine day the waters are constantly changing colours.

To reach the Blue Grotto itself (so called because of the deep blue of the water inside), boats pass under a natural arch, resembling a flying buttress. From here you glide into the dark grotto, 45m (50yds) deep into the cliffside.

2km (1¼ miles) southwest of Żurrieq. The charge for a trip is posted in the village.

With nature as the architect, the Blue Grotto is a cathedral in stone

Seen here on the horizon, the isle of Filfla has been declared a bird sanctuary

Filfla

Lying 5km (3 miles) off the south coast of Malta, this tiny rocky islet once served as a target for the guns of the British Navy and Royal Air Force. This practice devastated the island's birdlife, but since the islet was declared a bird sanctuary, the storm petrels, gulls and shearwaters have returned to breed. It is also home to a rare species of lizard. *No public access.*

Għar Lapsi

Not quite as pretty as it used to be, this is still one of the few spots on the south coast where you don't have to scramble down the cliffsides for a swim. It is also a very popular place for a picnic, with tables and benches laid out above the sea. Alternatively, there is a bar and sea-view restaurant serving local specialities. The water treatment plant nearby does not add to the attractions of the area, although it is doing a useful job in helping to solve Malta's water shortage. Known as a reverse-osmosis plant, it converts seawater to drinking water. *4km (2½ miles) south of Siġġiewi. Bus 94 from Siġġiewi in Jul & Aug, Thur & Sun.*

Ħaġar Qim and Mnajdra Archaeological Park

These twin temple complexes occupy a spectacular site above the sea, looking out to the island of Filfla. The sites date back to the Tarxien phases of around 3000–2500 BC, and there are a number of similarities with the Tarxien temples (*see pp106–7*).

Visiting the temples

A visit to the temples begins in a modern visitor centre with a film and exhibition telling the story of the sites and excavation. It is then a short walk to the Ħaġar Qim site and a further 500m (550yds) to the Mnajdra temple. The visitor centre has a ticket office, shop, café and toilets and was built with money from the European Union's regional development fund.

The approach to the temple site is a little disconcerting. The stones of Ħaġar Qim, once a landmark on top of a plateau, are now shrouded by a bright white dome resembling a landed spaceship. The stones were unearthed in 1839 and since then the surfaces of the soft limestone have suffered erosion from cycles of baking sun and winter rains. A solution was to cover the site with a high-tech fabric canopy. The same has been done to protect the neighbouring Mnajdra site.

The steep, dramatic cliffs of Għar Lapsi

The impressive megalithic stones of Ħaġar Qim

At first this may seem an eyesore, but it has had the benefit that once inside among the stones, the glare of the sun is subdued and it is possible to see more clearly the delicate surface designs. You get some sense that the temple is an enclosed sacred space which once had its own roof and it is more comfortable to spend time appreciating the site in the shade.

The canopy structures are so designed that the sides are open and at the solstice and equinox the sun's rays still light up parts of the temples that were sacred to the ancient people who worshipped there.

Ħaġar Qim

Ħaġar Qim means 'Standing Stones', and though the globigerina limestone has been badly eroded, especially on the seaward side, the site still retains megaliths of huge proportions. The largest is 7m by 3m (23ft × 10ft) which – with a block from the Ġgantija temples on Gozo – is the largest used in any of the temples.

When the site was excavated in the early 19th century, seven fat statuettes were found here, among them the so-called *Venus of Malta*, a headless clay figurine of a standing female nude of exceptionally generous proportions.

This is now in the National Museum of Archaeology (*see p42*), along with squatting stylised figures – also headless and extremely obese – and a four-sided limestone altar found in the temples.

The site is complex and irregular, made up of various chambers and passageways and with no obvious plan. Even so, it is a pleasure just to walk around and spot some of the details, such as the mushroom-shaped tables flanking one passageway, the shrine in the outer wall, the oval opening that suggests an oracle chamber, the blocks of stone covered with pitted decoration, and the well-designed temple façade.

Mnajdra temples

The setting of the Mnajdra temples, closer to the sea, is even more splendid and evocative than that of Ħaġar Qim. The three temples are protected by an outer wall of coralline limestone, which is harder than the globigerina variety and therefore better preserved than the stone of Ħaġar Qim. Similar features to Ħaġar Qim are the stone altars, the corbelling, and the square holes suggesting an oracular chamber. The whole façade of the Lower Temple is covered with pitted decoration.

The entrance to the park is 1.5km (1 mile) west of Qrendi, signposted off the main road. Tel: (356) 21424231. Open: summer daily 9am–7pm; winter daily 9am–5pm. Admission charge.

Marsaskala

Set at the head of a narrow, sheltered inlet, Marsaskala is steadily developing into a popular residential and tourist area for the Maltese. High-prowed, brightly painted *luzzus* (traditional boats) still dot the bay, but fishing is no longer its raison d'être. These days most restaurant owners in the village go to Marsaxlokk for the pick of the morning's catch.

South of Marsaskala, St Thomas Bay provides the only beach in the area but it is too small for the crowds, and rather overrun by modern development and holiday shacks.

Marsaskala is 11km (7 miles) southeast of Valletta. Bus 19 from Valletta (see p110).

Although Malta is a rocky and arid island, the soil still supports colourful blooms

The beach at Birżebbuġa provides calm and clear waters for swimming

Marsaxlokk Bay

Though Marsaxlokk itself still retains its fishing-village charm, the character of its landlocked bay has radically changed with the advent of the Malta Freeport. The inappropriately named Pretty Bay at Birżebbuġa now looks out to berthing facilities that cater annually for thousands of container ships.

Always a vulnerable inlet, Marsaxlokk Bay has seen the arrival of a number of enemy fleets over the centuries. It was here that Turkish galleys first arrived in 1565 at the start of the Great Siege. And it was here also that Napoleon and his troops landed in 1798, ending the Knights' rule on the island.

In December 1989 Marsaxlokk Harbour was the venue for the Bush/Gorbachev summit which symbolised the end of the Cold War. (The summit was going to take place in Valletta, but for security reasons it was transferred to a warship moored in Marsaxlokk Bay; the sea was so rough it was dubbed the 'Seasick Summit'!)

The charm of Marsaxlokk draws dozens of day-trippers, on either coach or boat excursions. Happily, though, the dearth of tourist accommodation has kept this very much a village rather than a resort.

Birżebbuġa

The town of Birżebbuġa, with its two bays, was developed as a summer resort for the Maltese long before the present tidal wave of tourism. Originally a fishing village, it now sprawls all the way from St George's Bay with its tiny beach, to Pretty Bay and Kalafrana beyond. The sandy beach at Pretty Bay is comparatively large for Malta, and still draws the crowds despite the proximity of the Malta Freeport.

The bars and restaurants of the town still thrive, but there is only one small hotel. For most visitors the main attraction is the fascinating cave of Għar Dalam (*see pp96–7*).
10km (6 miles) south of Valletta. Buses 11, 12 & 115 from Valletta.

Borġ in-Nadur

The fortified settlement of Borġ in-Nadur dates from the Bronze Age (around 1500–700 BC), and in ancient times consisted of a group of oval huts fortified by large ramparts. Only vestiges remain, but shallow, bottle-shaped pits, probably used for the storage of grain or water, were found close to the site on the edge of the seashore, some of them submerged. There are also cart tracks (*see p72*) leading directly into the sea.

The site is opened on request (*tel: (356) 22954000 to arrange a visit*). A word of caution: the remains are inconspicuous. To find them, you should go south of the main road junction at St George's Bay, then turn right between the bus stop and the public toilets. The first turning on the right will bring you to the remains.

Delimara

The long peninsula enclosing Marsaxlokk Bay on its eastern side runs down to Delimara Point where a lighthouse stands. This is popular walking territory, although less so since the construction of a power station on the Marsaxlokk Bay side. Its red-and-white-topped tower is a very conspicuous landmark. The bay spreads out below you, its waters intensely blue and inviting despite the spreading industrial sites. The seaward side of the peninsula remains unspoilt, and at Peter's Pool, signposted from the road, you can sunbathe on smooth rock shelves, or dive into deep clear waters.

The scenic bay of Marsaxlokk

North of Peter's Pool, Ħofra Iż-Żgħira and Ħofra I-Kbria are glorious horseshoe-shaped bays where the cliffs drop down to crystal-clear aquamarine-coloured waters. North of Ħofra I-Kbria, the remnants of a radio relay station dominate the headland, and a danger sign warns people with pacemakers to keep their distance. The peninsula is very popular with hunters, especially in the morning and early evening during spring and autumn, when migrating birds visit the island.

Għar Dalam

Għar Dalam, or the 'Cave of Darkness', gives its name to the first phase of Maltese prehistory (5000–4500 BC). The cave was one of the earliest sites used by Neolithic man, who crossed to the Maltese islands from Sicily around 5000 BC. Even more remarkable than the evidence of prehistoric man was the discovery of thousands of fossilised animal bones.

The cave was discovered in 1865 by an Italo-German palaeontologist. Excavations revealed that the floor of the cave had five different layers. In the lower layers were enormous quantities of fossilised bones, tusks and teeth belonging to extinct species – such as dwarf elephants and dwarf hippopotami – along with red deer, brown bears, wolves, foxes and giant swans. In the upper layers archaeologists found flint tools, sling-stones and pottery which had been decorated with the rippled edge of sea shells, or by pointed sticks or bones.

Basking in the sun at Peter's Pool

Long before archaeologists took any interest in this site, the remains of other prehistoric animals had been discovered elsewhere on the islands. Local Maltese believed they were the bones of the giants who were supposed to have built the islands' megalithic temples.

The Għar Dalam cave is a wide, low tunnel which cuts 140m (153yds) into the coralline limestone. Visitors can walk 80m (87yds) into the cave, aided by electric lighting, and there are useful explanations of what was discovered where. On the cave bed you can still see layers of bone deposits. At the entrance of the site a museum displays a fascinating collection of teeth, tusks and bones from the thousands of animals found here. Reconstructions show the size of extinct species such as the dwarf elephant. The more recently added display explains the formation of the cave and charts the animal and human finds.

The cave is signposted on the main Valletta–Birżebbuġa road, about 0.5km (¹/₃ mile) from St George's Bay. For information, tel: (356) 21675419. Open: daily 9am–5pm. Admission charge. Buses 11 & 115 from Valletta.

Kalafrana

Now dominated by container-terminal activities, Kalafrana used to be an important Royal Air Force (seaplane) base. Nearby is the disused Ħal Far airfield, used in World War II.

Ancient stalagmites and stalactites deep inside Għar Dalam, the 'Cave of Darkness'

Malta Freeport

The strategic location that Malta occupies within the Mediterranean, and its tax-free status, led to the establishment of the Malta Freeport in 1988. Marsaxlokk Harbour, being the biggest on the island, was the obvious choice for its location. Located on the main trade routes in the Mediterranean between Gibraltar and the Suez Canal, the Freeport has become a major hub for international business, linking markets across continents. Activities carried out within the tax-free zone include storage, packing, labelling, break-bulk, freezing and assembling.

The eye of Osiris

The most eye-catching feature of a Maltese fishing village is the *luzzu*, a small, high-prowed fishing boat painted in dazzling hues of red, blue, green and yellow. The boat may well have the name of a Catholic saint, but it will also be adorned, on either side of the prow, with the carved and painted eyes of a pagan god.

The custom of carving the ever-watchful eye, to ward off the devil and give protection to the little fishing boats, goes back centuries. The eye is that of Osiris, one of the most important gods of ancient Egypt. Legend has it that Osiris was drowned by the god Seth, who tore the corpse into 14 pieces and flung them over the earth. The goddess Isis found and buried the pieces, giving new life to Osiris. From then on he remained in the underworld as ruler of the dead, and as the power that grants all life, springing through the soil from the underworld. Egyptian dynastic rulers believed that they became one with Osiris at death, and thus became immortal.

Superstition is a strong characteristic of the Maltese. Some churches have two clocks on their belfries, one telling the correct time, the other falsely set to confuse the devil and distract him from his evil intent. Many farms and country houses have bulls' horns tied on the roof to ward off the devil, often alongside or close to a holy image. After all, most Maltese are, despite their devout Catholicism, the inheritors of pagan beliefs and traditions that long predate Christianity.

In order to spot Malta's traditional fishing boats, look in the harbours of St Julian's Bay, Marsaxlokk, and in the Blue Grotto. Off season you can see *luzzu* owners in the boatyards touching up the scratches, adding a lick of paint, or carefully defining that precious eye of Osiris.

Traditional *luzzus* have the painted eyes of a pagan god on the prow

Fishing boats on Malta add their colour to many a waterside scene

Marsaxlokk

Lying at the head of the deepest inlet of the bay, Marsaxlokk is the largest fishing village on the island. The name comes from the Arabic *marsa* meaning 'harbour', and *xlokk* – the local name for the hot, dry sirocco wind, which blows from the Sahara. You still sometimes hear the village called (or see it written as) Marsascirocco.

The first sight to catch your eye as you explore the village will be the fishing boats that bob in the blue waters of the bay, painted in an array of dazzling hues. On the quayside fishermen spread their nets, repair their fishtraps or touch up their boats for another day's work.

Adding to the colourful scene is the daily market, where lace and linen flutter in the breeze, and stalls are hung with chunky knitted jumpers. The main market day is Sunday, when the harbourside is packed with stalls selling everything from cacti and caged canaries to pirated CDs and funky T-shirts.

In season both Maltese and visitors arrive en masse, not just to buy at the market (the produce, apart from the fresh fish, is unremarkable), but to lunch out at one of Marsaxlokk's scores of restaurants. Naturally, the emphasis is on fish, and each restaurant is likely to offer a choice of a dozen different dishes, ranging from squid to swordfish. The wide range is sure to

The waterfront at Marsaxlokk

confuse you, but whatever you choose, it will certainly have a unique flavour. To eat here at the weekend, it is wise to reserve a table well in advance.
9km (5½ miles) south of Valletta. Bus 27 from Valletta.

Tas Silġ

In the 1960s, when Italian archaeologists excavated the Tas Silġ sanctuary, dedicated to the Phoenician goddess Astarte, they discovered not just Phoenician artefacts, but also, in the layers beneath, evidence of Bronze Age man. No one knows whether Malta was merely a convenient port of call for the Phoenicians, or whether they established a fully fledged settlement on the islands; in either case, the site provided the first evidence of probable coexistence between the prehistoric peoples already established on the islands and the Phoenician immigrants.
The ruins lie 1.5km (1 mile) east of Marsaxlokk, off the road going to Delimara Point, and can be visited on request. Tel: (317) 22954000. Admission charge.

Mqabba

Stone-quarrying is the main activity at Mqabba. Around here and Qrendi you can stop at the roadside and watch the limestone being cut before it is carted off to building sites. Thanks to the softness of the globigerina limestone, the blocks can be hewn using circular saws, eliminating any need for blasting. The great square holes, whose regular yellow walls look like slabs of cheese,

are an extraordinary sight. When the quarries are exhausted, the holes are filled with earth and sometimes used as vegetable plots. When one quarry closes, another has to open: limestone feeds the never-ending building boom in Malta. Piles of pale yellow stone can be seen all over Malta, either blocking pavements or stacked at roadsides.
10.5km (6½ miles) southwest of Valletta. Bus 35 from Valletta.

Paola

The town of Paola was officially established by Grand Master Antoine de Paule in 1626 to cope with the overspill from Valletta and the Three Cities. Today, it is a sprawling residential and commercial town which, with the notable exception of the Hypogeum and the temple ruins at neighbouring Tarxien, has little to delay the visitor.

Ħal Saflieni Hypogeum

In 1902, when builders were digging a well on a site for new houses in Paola, they struck the roof of the upper floor of a huge complex of underground chambers. Rather than reporting their discovery to the authorities, the builders used the cavity for the disposal of rubble. It was nearly three years before the existence of this vast and remarkable labyrinth of chambers became common knowledge. The excavations that subsequently took place were led by the eminent Maltese archaeologist Sir Themistocles Zammit.

The precise purpose of the Hypogeum remains a mystery, partially because of the primitive methods then available to the archaeologists; it is generally thought that the temple complex was used as a burial site and as a sanctuary. Archaeologists meanwhile dream of the discovery of another similar structure so that modern methods might throw light on the function of its individual features.

A tour of the Hypogeum is not really complete without a visit to the National Museum of Archaeology in Valletta (see p42), which has a model of the site, and a collection of the statuettes and pottery that were found here.

Tours of the site start with a brief exhibition and an audiovisual film focusing on the temple-builders and the relation of the site to above-ground prehistoric temples.

Covering nearly 800sq m (950sq yds), the chambers are on three levels down to a depth of 12m (39ft). Tools made of flint, bone and hard rock were used to hack at the limestone and create the chambers.

The highest level is the oldest, dating to around 3000 BC. From here, a modern spiral stairway leads down into the somewhat spooky centre of the complex (claustrophobics should steer clear). Here, the carved walls, corbelled ceilings, large three-stone doorways and fragments of spiral decoration all re-create the architectural features of the temples above ground. Because the ceilings here are intact, it gives you a good idea of how the above-ground temples (all now roofless) must have once looked.

The chamber known as the 'Holy of Holies' reveals traces of red ochre on the walls, red being the colour of blood, sacrifice and death, suggesting that this was both a burial place and a shrine. The Oracle Chamber, where a

One of the extraordinary underground chambers of the Hypogeum in Paola

square niche is cut into the wall, has remarkable acoustics. This is believed to be the cavity where the priest-oracle interpreted dreams. It was in these mid-level chambers that the so-called 'Sleeping Priestess' was discovered – a small statuette of a female with a tiny head and fat body lying on a couch. Other items found in the Hypogeum include pots with abstract decoration, and personal ornaments. From the middle level, an ancient and uneven staircase leads down to the lowest set of chambers. It was here, among the pits and tombs, that the remains of thousands of bodies were unearthed, along with their grave goods.

Triq Ħal-Saflieni (Burial St), Paola. Tel: (356) 21805019. Open daily for tours at 9am, 10am, 11am, 1pm, 2pm, 3pm & 4pm. To conserve the site the microclimate is strictly regulated and visitors are limited to a maximum of 80 a day, in small groups. Pre-booking is essential; at peak times this may be as much as two weeks in advance. To book online go to www.maltaticket.com; tickets are also available from the Hypogeum Visitor Centre or the National Museum of Archaeology in Valletta (see p42). No children under 6 allowed and those suffering from claustrophobia are advised against visiting. Admission charge. Buses 15, 29 & 30 from Valletta.

Qrendi

This ancient village of narrow twisting streets has no fewer than four churches and one tower. The village is within

Festive banners in the ancient and church-filled village of Qrendi

walking distance of the Blue Grotto and the temples of Ħaġar Qim and Mnajdra. Built by the Knights, the Gwarena Tower on Tower Road is unique in that it is the only octagonal tower to be found on the islands.

To the southeast of the village there is an extraordinarily large hole called **Il-Maqluba** which was created by the collapse of a series of caves. From a viewpoint you can look down on to the dense jungle of bamboo, bushes, carob and fruit trees that now fill the hole. As one of the few really fertile spots on the island, this is a mini-paradise for wildlife – and for the local children who collect the wild pomegranates.

11km (7 miles) southwest of Valletta. Bus 35 from Valletta.

The copperless Copper Age

Malta and Gozo are justly famous for their temples and tombs. On the two islands, 34 prehistoric sites have been discovered, 23 of them being temples. Some of these may, to the untrained eye, look no more than a pile of rubble or the tumbled remnants of a drystone wall. On the other hand, the finest examples demonstrate a remarkable sophistication, and rank among the oldest free-standing structures in the world.

A huge vessel found in an ancient temple

The first traces of civilisation on Malta date to around 5000 BC when farmers sailed across from Sicily. These first inhabitants lived in caves, but around 4000 BC a completely new way of life emerged. This was the era of the temple-builders – known, somewhat misleadingly, as the Copper Age. The tools used at this time were made of flint and obsidian – no copper was ever discovered.

The exact function of the temples remains a mystery, but the most likely theory is that they were built as places of worship as part of a fertility cult. The most eloquent evidence of this is the excavated statues and figurines of remarkably obese females, thought to represent a goddess of fertility. Some of these sculptures are so abstract as to look remarkably modern – as do some of the decorated pots that have been discovered along with them.

No two temples are the same, but all of them feature a series of horseshoe-shaped apses linked by a common passageway. A striking feature is the use of great monoliths, carefully crafted from limestone. These were probably transported by primitive sledges, carts, or pulleys and rollers. In this respect, the construction of the temples may be linked to Malta's famous prehistoric cart tracks (*see p72*).

Malta's temple-building civilisation came to a sudden end around 2000 BC. Nobody quite knows why; perhaps because of hostile invaders, the plague or famine. What is very apparent is that the race which followed was barbaric by comparison, and the disappearance of the temple-builders marked the end of the greatest phase of Maltese prehistory.

Prehistoric temples and sites, such as the Tarxien temples, continue to mystify and enthral visitors

Tarxien temples

The above-ground Tarxien temples provide a striking contrast to the dark subterranean chambers of the Hypogeum. This complex is the largest of the Copper Age temples on Malta. It is also the most elaborately embellished. As in the Hypogeum, no metal tools were used, and the ornamentation, in the form of spiral reliefs and carved animals, suggests a sophisticated community of temple-builders and carvers.

The complex was also the richest repository of prehistoric art on the islands, untouched for thousands of years, until Sir Themistocles Zammit started his excavations in 1915. To see the statuettes and ceramics discovered here, and for an overall appreciation of the complex, it is essential to visit the National Museum of Archaeology in Valletta (see p42). The site comprises three main temples, with a fourth in ruins. The age of the temples is a matter of some controversy, although it is generally believed that they were built between 3500 and 2500 BC.

The temple complex is entered through the threshold of the South Temple, which was restored in the 20th century. The large stone balls near the façade were used as rollers to transport the massive megaliths from which the temples were built. Inside the temple on the right is a statue of the lower half of a female figure, with a frilled skirt and obese legs. This is a copy of the original, which is preserved in the Museum of Archaeology. The statue, which must have originally stood nearly 3m (10ft) high and dominated the whole temple, is thought to have represented a fertility goddess. In the niches of this temple, bones and skulls of sacrificial animals were discovered, and still visible are the stones carved with a procession of what could be either sheep or goats. In the inner shrine a raised threshold, carved with an elaborate system of spirals, stands before the innermost part of the temple. Many of the decorations in the temple have been eroded by the elements, and the decorated blocks you see here are mainly replicas of those now in the archaeological museum.

The Middle Temple was a later addition, built between the South and East Temples. Thick layers of ash were discovered here when the temples were excavated, along with cinerary urns and burial offerings. Archaeologists are of the opinion that these were from the funeral pyres of late Bronze Age invaders, a cruder and fiercer race of people who made use of the temples long after the original Neolithic builders had disappeared into oblivion.

In a small room between the South and Middle Temples there are animal figures carved in relief on the walls. The two bulls and the sow suckling 13 piglets represent virility and fertility, the latter being a theme which constantly recurs within the temples. In the inner apses of the Middle Temple are more examples of spiral and pitted decorations.

The East Temple has what is believed to have been an oracle chamber. The secret hole in the wall was probably used by a priest or priestess. The acoustics here are exceptional. If you speak in a low voice through the niche, the sound of your voice will reverberate through the temple and even beyond it.

Triq it-Tempj Neolitici (Neolithic Temples St). The temples are located about 1km (⅔ mile) away from the Hal Saflieni Hypogeum (see pp101–3). Triq Sammet (Sammet St), north of the Hypogeum, leads to Triq it-Tempj Neolitici, near the entrance to the temples. Tel: (356) 21695578. Open: daily 9am–5pm. In summer go early to avoid the crowds and the midday sun (there is virtually no shade), and take bottled water. Admission charge. Buses 8, 11, 12 & 13 from Valletta.

The inner shrine, with its raised threshold carved with spirals

Żabbar

This old agricultural town, typically Maltese in character, began to prosper in the 17th century with the building of its huge parish church.

Hompesch Arch

Not nearly as distinguished as the Żabbar Gate, this arch, which acts as a roundabout, was the last monument to be built by the Knights. It is named after the last of the Order's Grand Masters, Ferdinand von Hompesch. *Southwest of Żabbar, on the road to Paola.*

Our Lady of Grace

The sanctuary was begun by the prolific architect Tommaso Dingli, although few of its original features survive today. The dome was badly damaged by French fire from the Cotonera Lines in 1800, aimed at Maltese insurgents who based themselves in Żabbar prior to attacking Valletta and the Three Cities. That dome was replaced with a fine new one which soars dramatically above the town. Suffering again in World War II, the church has since been restored to its former glory. A small museum contains ex-voto paintings offered by those who have escaped disasters at sea, including Maltese slaves who escaped from a Turkish galleon and, more recently, those who were miraculously saved when a bus plunged over the rocks.

Żabbar's church attracts many pilgrims and, on the eve of the *festa* of Our Lady of Grace, cyclists, motor-

TRANSPORT FROM VALLETTA

Żabbar is 8km (5 miles) southeast of Valletta. Buses 17, 18 & 19 from Valletta.

cyclists and motorists (in that order) make the journey from Rabat. *Tel: (356) 21824383. Open: daily 9am–noon. Museum open: Sun 9am–noon or by appointment. Donation appreciated.*

Żabbar Gate

The town is connected to the Three Cities by the triumphal Żabbar Gate, the finest of the gateways along the Cotonera Lines. The gate bears a bust of Grand Master Nicolas Cotoner (who funded the building of the Cotonera Lines), surrounded by a flurry of carved angels and war memorabilia. *On the Żabbar–Cospicua road.*

Żejtun

Żejtun means 'oil press', but nowadays there is not an olive tree in sight. However, this ancient town has retained two notable parish churches. The sombre and majestic Church of St Catherine, whose bold dome rises high above the town and its flat rural surroundings, is one of Lorenzo Gafà's finest achievements. It was built in 1692 and has been steadily embellished over the years. At one time it even earned itself the name 'Cathedral of the East'. The Church of St Gregory, situated on St Gregory's Road, is noticeably older and more mellow. It was built in 1436, then extended

The monumental Żabbar Gate carries a bronze bust of Grand Master Cotoner

by the Knights – hence the miscellany of styles.

8.5km (5¼ miles) south of Valletta. Buses 27, 28 & 29 from Valletta.

Żurrieq

This large, sprawling village and market centre is normally overlooked by visitors in a hurry to get to the Blue Grotto. It is one of the oldest villages in Malta and several of its buildings date from the days of the Knights. The Church of St Catherine boasts some of the finest paintings by Mattia Preti, who lived here in 1675; sadly, like so many church paintings in Malta, these are too dark to appreciate fully.

On the edge of the village the small Armeria Palace, with a watchtower at the rear, was built by the Knights and used as an armoury. In the abandoned settlement of Ħal Millieri, the late medieval Church of the Annunciation has been restored by the local conservation society. In addition to its importance as a historic village, Żurrieq is famous for its two summer *festas*. The festivities last several days with long processions through the streets, and huge sums of money are spent on spectacular displays of fireworks.

10.5km (6½ miles) southwest of Valletta. Bus 32 from Valletta.

Tour: Southern Malta

Variety is the keynote – this tour takes in temples, fishing villages and coastal grottoes. The round trip totals 64km (40 miles).

Allow a full day.

From Sliema, follow the coast road south; after Msida Creek, at a major junction, follow the signs for Birkirkara (marked B'kara), then turn left at the Hospital sign. Follow the airport signs to Paola.

1 Paola

Here you can see Malta's most famous prehistoric site: the Hypogeum (*see pp101–3*).

From Paola head east to Żabbar, via the Hompesch Arch (see p108), and follow the signs to Marsaskala.

2 Marsaskala

Marsaskala (*see p93*) has no sandy beach, but you can swim from the rocks or sit in a café and watch the fishing boats. On the headland, opposite a derelict hotel, stands the forbidding St Thomas Tower, built by the Knights in 1614, following a Turkish incursion.

Take the main road south from Marsaskala (marked St Thomas Bay); turn first right, then left (marked to Marsaxlokk), then follow the signs to Delimara Point.

3 Delimara Peninsula

Despite the power station (built in front of Dom Mintoff's seaside retreat) and the activities of the Malta Freeport, Delimara Peninsula still makes a spectacular vantage point. Peter's Pool, marked from the road, is an idyllic spot in which to swim off the rocks.

Retrace your route from Delimara Point, and turn left at the small, green-domed chapel for Marsaxlokk.

4 Marsaxlokk

Stop for lunch at Malta's most picturesque fishing village – either a bite on the harbourfront, or fresh fish cooked Maltese style.

Continue round the bay down into St George's Bay. Turn right here for the Għar Dalam cave (see pp96–7). Continuing around the bay, stop at the monument on the seafront opposite the Pinto Battery.

5 Gorbachev/Bush Monument

A monument opposite the Pinto Battery commemorates the summit on board a ship anchored in Marsaxlokk Bay between Presidents Gorbachev and George Bush on 3 December 1989. This meeting effectively ended the Cold War. *Follow the coast road round to Pretty Bay. At the entrance to the Malta Freeport bear right. Skirt the disused Ħal Far airfield. Turn left at the junction and bear right along a secondary road into Żurrieq. At the main road turn left, following signs for the Blue Grotto and Wied iż-Żurrieq.*

6 Blue Grotto

Before Wied iż-Żurrieq a roadside 'balcony' affords magnificent views over the sea and cliffs. Boats for the Blue Grotto (*see pp88–9*) depart from the harbour of Wied iż-Żurrieq.

Leaving Wied iż-Żurrieq, rejoin the main road, turning left through barren hilly countryside, and divert left for the spectacularly sited Ħaġar Qim and Mnajdra temples (see pp90–93). After 3km (1¾ miles) turn left at a roundabout for Għar Lapsi.

7 Għar Lapsi

End the day at this cove and tiny beach beneath the cliffs. A restaurant serves the Maltese national dish of *fenek* (stewed rabbit).

Return to the roundabout, and make the home journey passing by the church-dominated villages of Siġġiewi and Żebbuġ. From Żebbuġ, follow the signs for Valletta, then for Marsa and Sliema.

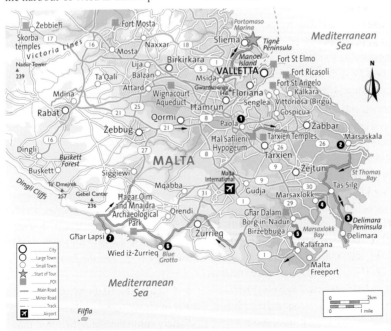

Tour: Southern Malta

Northern Malta

Northern Malta has a varied and heavily indented coastline. Until the British came, the whole area was more or less uninhabited. Coastal attacks had forced the islanders to form their communities inland, and the only structures of any significance were the coastal watch-towers built by the Knights. St Paul's is one of the region's few settlements, and in recent years it has grown from being a humble fishing village into a great hub of tourism.

St Paul's was once a weekend retreat for the Maltese, who cut boathouses out of the rocks and built holiday homes. Now the development stretches, almost uninterrupted, for over 5km (3 miles) along the bay. The most heavily developed area is Buġibba, which, with its big apartment blocks and general air of tourism, resembles one of the Spanish costas. Other stretches of the north are still unspoilt. Between Baħar iċ-Ċagħaq and Salina Bay, the only structures along the craggy coastline are a couple of towers. In summer cars park along the coast road, and the rocks are dotted with swimmers or people picnicking by the sea. Inland the scenery is noticeably barren, the only conspicuous plants being the agaves bowing to the wind.

Another quiet and seemingly remote region is Marfa Ridge, whose tip forms the northernmost part of Malta. The only developments here are the small resorts on the Comino side, where low-rise Maltese holiday homes dot small, sandy bays. The west coast has the loveliest and least-spoilt scenery: golden, sandy bays separated by rugged headlands, cliffs providing fine walks, and fertile valleys where you can still see horse-drawn carts and women hoeing in the fields. Drystone walls flank neat, sloping fields of vegetables and vines, while the paths are strewn with wild fennel and caper bushes.

Għajn Tuffieħa

Għajn Tuffieħa is the name of the rugged stretch of coast west of Mġarr, where three golden bays and a backdrop of spectacular cliffs combine to form Malta's most desirable coastline. There is very little development, and the hinterland is noticeably green in comparison to the rest of the island.

Għajn Tuffieħa Bay is 3.5km (2¼ miles) northwest of Mġarr. Buses 47 & 52 from Valletta.

Sheltered coves and blue sea make Malta a tourist paradise

Għajn Tuffieħa Bay

This is the largest and the most beautiful of the three bays. The steps down the cliffside and the limited facilities deter many beachgoers, and it is never as crowded as Golden Bay. A watchtower stands on the promontory to the north, and a derelict hotel overlooks the beach. Southwards there are fine walks along the cliffs (*see pp120–21*).

Ġnejna Bay

Approached from the Mġarr road, the smallest of the three bays is easily reached by car. It is another pretty bay, although the sands here are more shingly and the boathouses don't enhance the setting. If the beach is crowded, make for the rocks to the north, which are sufficiently smooth for sunbathing. From the bay the road to Mġarr passes through the pretty Ġnejna Valley, a fertile area where figs, bamboo and vines flourish.

Golden Bay (Ramla Tal-Mixquqa)

Golden sands, aquamarine waters and ease of access make this the most popular of the three beaches. In summer months expect to step over bronzing bodies to find a spare patch of sand. A good many of them will be staying at the huge new Radisson Blu (SAS) Golden Sands Resort, which lies north of the bay.

This is a good family beach where you can windsurf, waterski, tour on an inflated 'sea-sausage', ride a horse to the Popeye Village or take a speedboat or cruiser to Comino's Blue Lagoon. The shallow, clear waters are very tempting, but take heed if the warning flags are flying.

The Popeye Village film set at Anchor Bay

Mellieħa and environs

Perched high on a spur, the town of Mellieħa (Maltese for 'salt pans') overlooks a sweeping expanse of bay and beach. It is a busy shopping centre with more character than the resorts to its east. The steep main street, lined with shops, bars and restaurants, caters for residents as well as holidaymakers. Mellieħa has a range of self-catering accommodation, including luxury villas (one area with sea views is known as Millionaire's Valley). At the other extreme is a vamped-up cave dwelling above the road which zigzags down to the beach. One of several caves inhabited by troglodytes in the past, it was used as a bomb shelter in World War II.

Somewhat cut off from the island's main activity centres, the village and the little resorts of Marfa Ridge are well suited to those seeking relative peace, good walks, excellent swimming and boat trips to Gozo and Comino.

13km (8 miles) northwest of Rabat. Buses 43, 44 & 45 from Valletta.

Church of Our Lady of Victories

The large parish church of Mellieħa stands sentinel over the bay, perched on a spur. Below it the fascinating Grotto of the Madonna is an intimate little marble chapel with an ancient fresco of the Virgin Mary. The locals claim it was painted by St Luke. In a side corridor there are numerous votive offerings to Our Lady in thanksgiving for cures and miracles. The spring water in the Grotto is said to have medicinal powers.
Mellieħa Square. Open: Mon–Fri 8.30am–noon & 4–6pm. Free admission.

Għadira Nature Reserve

In an effort to preserve both local and migratory birds from Malta's merciless hunters, the wetland inland from Mellieħa Bay has been turned into a bird sanctuary. It lies 100m (110yds) from Mellieħa Bay, across the main road, and covers around 6 hectares (15 acres). Over 200 species have been recorded. Resident species to look out for are black-winged stilts, avocets and Cetti's warblers. Among the migratory birds seen here are plovers, little stints, ruffs, redshanks, greenshanks and various interesting types of sandpiper. *Tel: (356) 21347646. www.birdlifemalta. org. Open: Nov–May Sat & Sun 10am– 4pm. Volunteers lead guided walks. Free admission. Donations welcome.*

Marfa Ridge

If you see Malta as a fish, Marfa Ridge is the tail. Here the sea views, the small sandy beaches and – for Malta – the surprising amount of greenery combine to make excellent walking territory (*see pp122–3*). From **Ċirkewwa**, ferries sail across to Gozo, passing the little island of Comino on the way. You can sit either on deck or inside the cafeteria.

Ċirkewwa is also one of the departure points for boats to Comino. These are more like fishing boats than ferries – and the boatmen often trail a line through the waters as the boat crosses the channel.

South of Ċirkewwa, **Paradise Bay** has an attractive but small and usually crowded sandy bay. *Ċirkewwa is 5.5km (3¹/₂ miles) northwest of Mellieħa. Bus 45 from Valletta.*

Mellieħa Bay

Two kilometres (1¹/₄ miles) north of the town, and also known as Għadira Bay, this is the biggest sandy beach on Malta. Extensive sands and good beach facilities draw the crowds through the whole season from spring to autumn. It is one of the best beaches for children, as it slopes very gently. Watersports enthusiasts are well catered for, with paragliding, windsurfing, waterskiing, sailing and canoeing. The drawbacks are that there is a busy main road running behind the beach, and that the beach gets crowded in summer. *1.5km (1 mile) northwest of Mellieħa.*

Popeye Village

The Popeye, or Sweethaven, Village at **Anchor Bay** was built as the set for Robert Altman's 1980 film *Popeye*. The ramshackle village by the sea consists of 17 houses, all of them made of wood imported from Canada and the Netherlands. Amenities include a souvenir shop, snack bar, beach facilities, a small fun park, and you can even see a film about the making of *Popeye*. Boat trips are available during the summer at no additional charge. *2.5km (1¹/₂ miles) west of Mellieħa at Anchor Bay. Tel: (356) 21524782. www.popeyemalta.com. Open: Mar–Oct daily 9.30am–5.30pm (Aug 7pm); Nov–Feb Mon–Fri 9.30am–4.30pm. Admission charge.*

Mġarr

The dominant feature of this village is its huge 'Egg Church' (*see p121*). On the same square, at Restaurant Barri, you can try a *fenkata*, or rabbit meal, for which Mġarr is renowned.

6km (3¾ miles) northwest of Mosta. Bus 47 from Valletta.

Skorba temples

Tall megalithic blocks and scanty ruins mark the site of one of Malta's very earliest settlements. Excavations here in the 1960s revealed that Neolithic man had built a small village of huts, which were made of wattle-and-daub and set on low stone foundations. This is the only such settlement on Malta that has been fully investigated.

There are also the fragmentary ruins of two later temples, which were probably once roofed over. Various types of pottery found on the site gave their names to the Red Skorba phase (4400–4100 BC) and the Grey Skorba phase (4500–4400 BC). Pots, vases and fragments of figurines unearthed here can be seen in the National Museum of Archaeology in Valletta (*see p42*).

1.5km (1 mile) east of Mġarr, on the outskirts of Żebbieħ. Tel: (356) 21580590 to arrange a visit. Open: Tue 11.30am–1pm or on request. Admission charge.

Ta'Ħaġrat temples

These two prehistoric temples are similar to those of Skorba, though they are not quite as old. However, the remains are scanty, and of real interest only to experts and enthusiasts.

In Mġarr, signposted off the road to Mosta. Tel: (356) 21586264 to arrange a

visit. Open: Tue 9.30–11am or on request. Admission charge.

St Paul's Bay (San Pawl il-Baħar)

Several sites around this bay recall stories of St Paul's sojourn in Malta. **Għajn Rasul (Apostle's Fountain)**, on the coastal road, is said to be the spot where St Paul struck a rock – which promptly spouted water. Meanwhile, the parish Church of St Paul (Our Lady of Sorrows) is supposed to stand on the site of the spot where St Paul shook off a viper into the fire.

St Paul's itself sprawls along the main coastal road. Though it is not as blatantly tourist-oriented as Buġibba (*see p118*), it has lost much of its former fishing-village charm, and its older buildings look somewhat forlorn. The prettiest spot is the harbour,

ST PAUL'S SHIPWRECK

According to the Acts of the Apostles (Chapter 27), St Paul and St Luke were on their way to Rome to be tried as political rebels when their ship foundered on the rocks of Malta. The actual site of the shipwreck is generally thought to have been one of the islets to the north of St Paul's Bay. The Apostles were welcomed by the islanders, and for an entire winter they sheltered in a cave at Rabat. It was from here that St Paul preached the Gospel, converting the Roman governor, Publius, who later became the first Bishop of Malta.

The islet of Selmunett is today distinguished by a huge statue of St Paul. The island is uninhabited, but you can hire a boat or swim across for a closer look – it is only about 200m (220yds) from St Paul's Bay. Once a year the Maltese sail over to celebrate open-air Mass by the statue.

Relaxing by St Paul's Bay

though even here the view of fishing boats is gradually giving way to one of modern construction.

Nearby, the **Wignacourt Tower**, housing The Island Fortress exhibition, is one of the few reminders of the days of the Knights. A more modern landmark on the seafront is the Gillieru restaurant, where boats draw up for some of the best fish and sea views in the region.

17km (10½ miles) northwest of Valletta. Buses 43, 44, 45 & 49 from Valletta.

Sheltered waters encourage a variety of watersports

late Pope John Paul II, who came to Malta in 1990.

Underwater Safari tel: (356) 23463333. www.captainmorgan.com.mt. Open: May–Oct, four times a day from Buġibba's il-Menqa, next to Bognor Beach. Reservations can be made through hotels or any travel agent or through **Captain Morgan Cruises**, *Dolphin Court, Tigné Seafront, Sliema. Bus 49 from Valletta to Buġibba, bus 70 from Sliema or Buġibba.*

Buġibba

The architecture is hardly very inspiring, but Buġibba is probably the cheapest place on the island to stay. Although somewhat cut off from Valletta and from the main parts of the island, its facilities are such that many of its visitors are happy to stay put. The emphasis is on bars, pubs, discos and restaurants (mainly of the pasta, pizza and hamburger variety). A lively promenade offers bathing and a variety of watersports, including paragliding. On summer evenings the streets are crowded with people, and music blares from late-night bars.

Daytime activities include boat trips to the islands of Comino and Gozo. Another popular tour is the **Underwater Safari**; as you steam around St Paul's Bay portholes below sea level allow you to view the world of marine fauna and flora, as well as a couple of shipwrecks. There are also views from the boat of the statue of Christ, commemorating the visit of the

Mistra Bay

This sheltered inlet on the northern side of St Paul's Bay affords good swimming from the rocks. It is also a popular spot for dog owners to take their pets for a swim, which is great fun if you like dogs, but otherwise you might want to stay away.

Qawra

Together, Qawra and Buġibba now occupy almost the entire peninsula on the east side of St Paul's Bay. More or less merging with Buġibba, Qawra is more restrained than its noisy neighbour, with a choice of slightly superior accommodation.

Hotels and apartment buildings have been mushrooming here since the 1970s. Among the hotels is the Dolmen Resort, named after the prehistoric remains that stand in its gardens.

Like Buġibba, there are lots of bars, cafés and restaurants. The rocky beach has a restaurant, and lots of watersports enthusiasts flock here to

enjoy the resort. The Qawra Tower at the far end of the peninsula was one of many fortress towers erected by Grand Master Martin de Redin during the 17th century.
Buses 49, 57 & 449 from Valletta.

Salina Bay

East of St Paul's Bay, Salina Bay cuts deeply into the coastline, and at the head of the bay there are salt pans. They look like shallow trays cut into the stone, and were created by the Knights in the 17th century. The west side of the bay is dominated by the high-rise development of Qawra, which includes the Suncrest Hotel, the largest resort hotel in the area.

Splash and Fun Park/ Mediterraneo Marine Park

Malta's two main leisure parks are set side by side on the north coast. The Splash and Fun Park provides water chutes, a large wave pool, lazy river and playground with dinosaurs. The Mediterraneo Marine Park has dolphin, sea lion and parrot shows and a children's play area. Children over 8 years old can swim with the dolphins (extra charge) – a big attraction but a costly one at €120. There are also a reptile house and seals.
Baħar iċ-Ċagħaq, 9km (5½ miles) northwest of Valletta. Splash and Fun Park tel: (356) 21374283. www.splashandfun.com.mt. Open: Apr–Sept daily 10am–7pm (later in high season).
Mediterraneo Marine Park tel: (356) 21372218. www.mediterraneo.com.mt. Open: daily 10am–5pm; closed for a few weeks in Jan & Feb, phone to check. Admission charge to both.
Bus 68 from Valletta, bus 70 from Buġibba or Sliema.

Value for money is an important part of Buġibba's appeal

Walk: Għajn Tuffieħa seascapes

Għajn Tuffieħa is hard to beat for cliff scenery and dazzling blue seas. This walk follows the cliff tops, then turns inland to the village of Mġarr, where you can lunch on rabbit stew. You can complete the circuit either by walking along the road or by taking a bus to Valletta. The full walk is a circuit of 8km (5 miles).

Allow 2 hours.

Start at the Radisson Blu (SAS) Golden Sands Resort at Ramla Tal-Mixquqa (Golden Bay. Bus 47 or 52 from Valletta). Take the track to the cliff top and follow the path to the tower on the headland.

1 Għajn Tuffieħa

At the headland stop to savour the magnificent seascape of Għajn Tuffieħa. It was here in 1565 that 181 Turkish ships lay at anchor, awaiting a change of wind before landing at Marsaxlokk. The

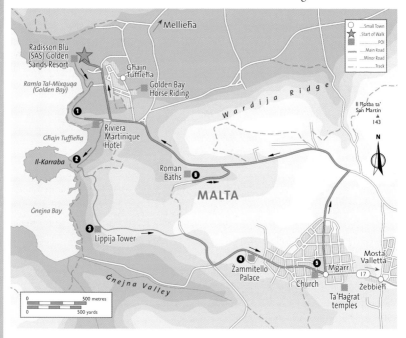

beach of Għajn Tuffieħa is arguably the loveliest on Malta.

Follow the path round to the car park above the beach. Beyond the derelict Riviera Martinique Hotel take the path to the right over the cliffs. Keep to the ridge all the way, avoiding the path lower down the cliffs.

2 Il-Karraba

The sea has chiselled weird and wonderful geological features along this coast. Il-Karraba (the Battleship) is the name given to the prominent, strange-shaped headland; 'Dinosaur' is the ridge which gives access to it.

Keep to the ridge. The occasional outcrop may divert you, but try to walk along the coast as far as possible.

3 Lippija Tower

When Ġnejna Bay comes into view, head for the tower, which stands slightly inland. This was one of several watch-towers built to defend the coast against Turkish attacks.

Lippija Tower overlooks idyllic golden sands

Just before the tower, pick up a rough track leading inland, with views over the Ġnejna Valley. Turn right when you reach a narrow metalled road, and follow it for 0.5km (¹/₃ mile). At the minor crossroads turn left for Mġarr.

4 Żammitello Palace

Home of the Sant Cassia family, this elegant little mansion is now a wedding and function hall.

Continue down the same road.

5 Mġarr

The disproportionately large church was funded from the sale of poultry and eggs – hence the ovoid shape of the dome. Off the road to Mosta, signed from the square, you can visit the Ta'Ħaġrat temples (*see p116*).

From Mġarr, take bus 47 back to Valletta. Alternatively, return to Golden Bay by foot using the roads. Take the left turn beyond the church, and after 1km (²/₃ mile) turn left again towards Għajn Tuffieħa. Continue until you see, on the left, a complex of ancient ruins.

6 Roman Baths

Although the house is in ruins, the baths are relatively well presented and include relics of the steam baths, water channels, lavatories, changing rooms, swimming pool and mosaics. Visit by appointment with Heritage Malta (*tel: (356) 22954000, email: info@heritagemalta.org*).

After 1km (²/₃ mile) turn left at the junction, then right for Golden Bay.

Walk: Marfa Ridge

This exposed ridge of northern Malta provides fine seascapes, cool breezes, and sufficient shade from trees and shrubs to shelter you from the midday sun.

Allow 3 hours for this 9km (5½-mile) walk.

Start at the Armier crossroads, which you can reach by taking bus 45 to Ċirkewwa from Valletta. If you are coming from Mellieħa, look for the landmark tower southwest of the crossroads.

1 The Red Tower

On the crest of the Marfa Ridge, the gaunt, weathered tower was built by Grand Master Lascaris in the mid-17th century to guard against pirate raids and the possible return of the Turks.

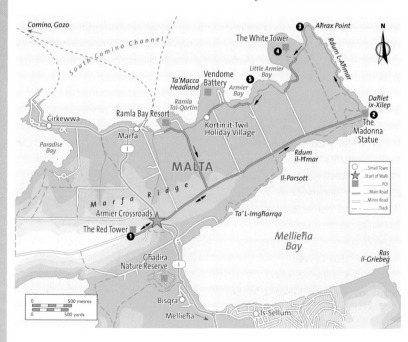

It was used by the British as a signal station in World War II.

Open: Mon–Sat & first Sun of the month 10am–1pm, but varies. Free admission.

From the crossroads take the potholed ridge road that runs to the northeast.

2 The Madonna Statue

The end of the ridge road is marked by a lonely Madonna and a tiny chapel, built to replace an older one that is now in ruins. On fine days ramblers picnic among the pines, and homing-pigeon enthusiasts release their birds. Out to sea you can normally spot at least one huge tanker on the horizon, or the ferry sailing between Sa Maison and Gozo.

Turn left and walk along the headland, carefully making your way over the rough coralline limestone, scattered with tiny, white snail shells. The cliffs gradually give way to a less dramatic rocky shoreline, from where fishermen cast out their lines into the vivid blue waters.

3 Aħrax Point

The most northerly tip of Malta. Beware of the great oval cavernous hole, about 25m long and 14m wide (27yds × 15yds), whose depths are filled with dark-looking waters.

From here walk south, heading towards the White Tower.

4 The White Tower

The tower and the redoubts punctuating the coast used to be the only structures on Marfa Ridge. Today, the bays on this side of the ridge are dotted with Maltese holiday homes.

Work your way along the coast, savouring the sea views and stopping for a dip at one of the sandy bays.

5 Armier Bay

The two sandy crescents of this bay have become quite popular during the summer, when you will find beach facilities, pedalos for hire and a few simple cafés.

At the end of Armier Beach, beyond the car park, turn left; then, where the main road bends, go straight on, thereby cutting across the Ta'Macca headland. Skirt the small beach of Ramla Tal-Qortin, passing some boathouses, and continue on to the Ramla Bay Resort. The views from here across to Comino and Gozo are superb. Retrace your route around the bay to the minor road leading south to the ridge road, then turn right to return to your starting point.

The Red Tower on Marfa Ridge, built as a lookout for pirates

Tour: Northern Malta

This 60km (37-mile) tour takes you along the varied coast of northern Malta, round bays, over ridges and down to the golden sands of the west coast.

Allow a full day and be prepared for traffic jams, especially on summer Sundays.

From Sliema follow the coast road to St Julian's, where Spinola Bay is studded with fishing boats. Going up the hill follow the signs for St Andrew's, and join the main road. Rejoin the coast again at Baħar iċ-Ċagħaq, where the water chutes of the Splash and Fun Park catch the eye. The road then follows an undeveloped stretch of coastline.

1 Salina Bay

Rounding Għallis Point, where a lonely tower stands guard over Salina Bay, the modern blocks on the far side hit the eye. Skirt the salt pans at the head of the inlet, and, just after the bay, stop at the Kennedy Memorial Grove. Here, a simple, evocative monument, standing among trees and shrubs, commemorates the assassination of United States President John F Kennedy in 1963.
Follow the signs to St Paul's Bay, and reach the harbour by turning right after the petrol station. At the harbour take a left turn, keeping to the coast, and stop at the coastal tower.

2 Wignacourt Tower

Grand Master Wignacourt was responsible for this and many other early 17th-century towers. It was renovated in 1997, and now contains a small military museum. From here there are good views of St Paul's Islands, where the Apostle was shipwrecked.
Take the fourth street on the left to rejoin the main road. Turn right and follow the road down to Pwales Beach. Climb up through Xemxija, down into the Mistra Valley, and zigzag up towards Mellieħa. Before the village, turn right at a roundabout marked Selmun Palace.

3 Selmun Palace

This fortified villa was built in the 18th century as a country retreat. Today, it is used for social functions and as a restaurant. In the grounds of the palace is the four-star Grand Hotel Selmun Palace Mercure, which echoes the palace in style. There are fine walks over the headland, and, if you take the track opposite the chapel and scramble down the cliffside, you will find a delightful hidden beach.

4 Mellieħa

Rejoin the main road to Mellieħa. Stop to see the church (*see p114*) and the nearby air-raid shelters built during World War II and one of the largest shelter complexes on Malta.

Zigzag down to the large beach of Mellieħa. The same road will take you to Marfa Ridge. Turn right along the ridge road and drive until you can go no further. Stop by the Madonna for splendid seascapes, then return to the roundabout on the far side of Mellieħa's beach, and take the steep, twisting, wide road uphill marked Għajn Tuffieħa.

When you reach the next roundabout take the rough road to the right.

5 Għajn Tuffieħa

Scenically, this is the best part of the tour. A huge sweep of the west coast with its cliffs and fertile hinterland comes into view as you approach Għajn Tuffieħa. Crops, vegetables and grapevines flourish on the valley slopes, creating, along with the drystone walls, the effect of a colourful patchwork.

Choose Golden Bay or Għajn Tuffieħa for a swim or a walk along the sands, then take the inland road to Żebbieħ. From there, follow the signs for Mosta, whose dome looms above the village. Return to Sliema following the signs to Valletta, Msida and, finally, Sliema.

Tour: Northern Malta

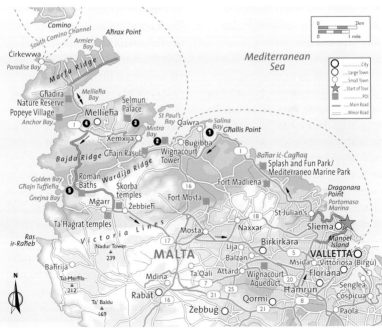

Gozo

Lying just 6km (3¾ miles) off the coast of northern Malta, Gozo looks like a smaller version of its sister island. In some ways it is. The fields sheltered by stone walls, the flat-roofed houses and the blue waters surrounding the island are all reminiscent of Malta. At the same time it is noticeably more peaceful and rural, the pace of life is slower, the land is greener, the streets are cleaner and the coast is quieter.

Gozo was, for centuries, the victim of marauding Arabic and Turkish pirates. Gozitans were often killed or taken off into slavery, leaving the population much depleted. Unlike Malta, Gozo has not made a living from trade. Farming (and to a lesser extent fishing) has always been the main activity of the islanders. That is why the villages were tightly packed on the hilltops. It left the slopes and valleys for intensive cultivation of vegetables and fruit. The irregular-shaped plots still necessitate simple methods of farming. Donkey carts, primitive ploughs and field workers wielding hoe and scythe are part of the charm of the landscape.

Flat-topped hills and Baroque domes dominate the skyline. The houses in the villages have strikingly ornate features – whether they are old buildings with finely carved balconies, or new ones with twisted columns or ornate carvings.

Getting around Gozo presents no difficulty. All roads radiate from the capital, Victoria, and the signposting is

good. Most visitors come for the day from Malta, taking in Victoria (whose handsome citadel sits on a hill at the island's centre), the finely preserved prehistoric temples of Ġgantija, and the fishing villages of Xlendi or Marsalforn. Those who choose to stay on here and explore its coastline and landscape will discover there is far more to the island than these well-known spots.

Malta's little sister now has half a dozen upmarket hotels, including the Kempinski Hotel San Lawrenz, an exclusive resort and spa. Farmhouses have been converted into luxury accommodation, stylish restaurants have opened and seaplanes now provide speedy, stylish access from Valletta. However, development has been discreet and this small unspoilt island – still essentially one of fishing and farming – manages to retain its simple charm.
(*For details of ferry and seaplane services from Malta to Gozo,* see pp185–6.)

Gozo and Comino

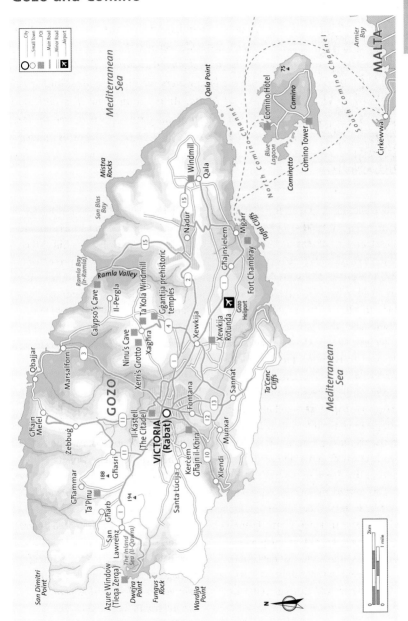

VICTORIA (RABAT)

The capital and the hub of the island, Victoria combines an impressive hilltop citadel and a lively town below. The name was given to the city in 1897, on the occasion of Queen Victoria's jubilee, but to the Gozitans – and many Maltese – it will always be Rabat; that name means 'suburb' and, as with Mdina and Rabat on Malta, the town here is a suburb of the fortress. Although enjoyable for a day visit, do not reckon on staying here: there is only one hotel in Victoria, and few places to eat at night.

Il-Kastell (The Citadel)

Crowning a flat-topped hill, the great bastions of the citadel dominate central Gozo, sheltering within its walls the cathedral and several museums.

The bastions date from the early 17th century, funded by King Philip II of Spain and the Gozitans by means of a levy on wine, oil and other comestibles. The Knights refortified the ramparts and used the citadel as a refuge against attacks by Turks and pirates. At one time the entire population of Gozo was able to shelter within its walls.

An earthquake in 1693 reduced much of the citadel to rubble. Today, the bastions are undergoing restoration with the aid of UNESCO.

Archaeological Museum
(Palazzo Bondi)

The 17th-century Palazzo Bondi makes a fitting setting for Gozo's archaeological finds. Exhibits range from fragments of prehistoric pots to Roman amphorae and pottery found on shipwrecks off the coast of Gozo. The museum has a model of the Ġgantija prehistoric temples (*see pp138–9*) and excavated finds from the site, including a stone phallus.
Triq Bieb il-Mdina. Tel: (356) 21556144.
Open: daily 9am–5pm.
Admission charge.

Cathedral

The fine classical façade of the cathedral, raised above a flight of steps, makes a powerful impact as you step inside the citadel. The cathedral was designed by Lorenzo Gafà, and built between 1697 and 1711 to replace an earlier church destroyed by the 1693 earthquake. It is one of the best examples of Baroque vernacular architecture in Malta, and was the Knights' own conventual church on Gozo; on two occasions it served as the venue for the sumptuous investitures of the Grand Masters.

Compared with the relatively restrained exterior, the inside is very ornate. Tombstones decorate the nave floor, and Baroque paintings cover the walls of the side chapels – but the most fascinating aspect is the *trompe-l'œil* painting which very convincingly (at least from the nave) creates the illusion of a large dome. The roof, as you can see from the ramparts, is, in fact, flat. Funds were insufficient for a real dome so, in 1732, the Italian artist Antonio Manuele of Messina was commissioned to paint a false one.

The statue of Santa Marija (left, as you enter the church) was originally selected in Rome as a statue suitable for parading along the streets during local *festas*. When the Madonna arrived from Rome it is said that 'the people wept in satisfaction'. In 1956 the statue was formally donated to the cathedral and embellished with a diamond necklace, a solid gold belt and, six years later, a solid silver plinth.

So highly regarded was the statue that a large modern arch was cut into the city wall in 1956 to make room for her entry into the citadel.

Pjazza Katidral (Cathedral Square).
Tel: (356) 21554101. Open: Mon–Sat 9am–5pm, Sun for services.
Free admission.

TRANSPORT FROM MĠARR

Bus 25 from Mġarr Harbour to Victoria.

Victoria (Rabat)

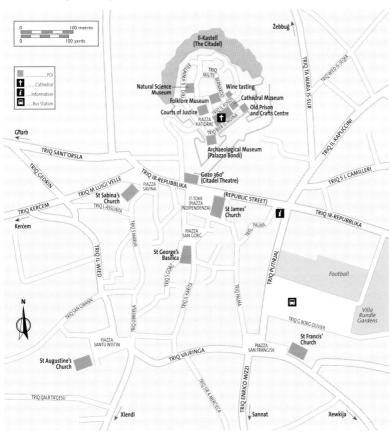

The impressive façade of Gozo's cathedral

Cathedral Museum

At the back of the cathedral, this museum houses a modest collection of vestments, religious paintings, church ornamentation and old manuscripts. There is also a horse-drawn carriage which was used by the Bishop of Gozo on special occasions in the 19th century. *Triq il-Fosos (Fosse St). Tel: (356) 21556087. Open: Mon–Sat 10am–4.30pm, Sun 8.30am–3pm. Admission charge.*

Crafts Centre

This is a permanent and extensive display of Gozitan crafts in the old prison buildings. *Citadel. Tel: (356) 21556160. Free admission.*

Folklore Museum

This is a charming museum where exhibits are laid out in the rooms of three late medieval houses. The emphasis is on everyday Gozitan life over the centuries. The exhibits cover crafts, costumes and farming tools. *Triq Milite Bernardo (off Triq il-Fosos). Tel: (356) 21562034. Open: daily 9am–5pm. Admission charge.*

Gozo 360°

This multivision show gives a dramatic glimpse into Gozo's past and present. *Citadel Theatre. Tel: (356) 21559955. Shows: Mon–Sat every half-hour 10.30am–4.30pm. Admission charge.*

Natural Science Museum

The small exhibition on the geology and marine life of the island includes displays of fossils, fish and coral. *Triq il-Kwartier (Quarters St). Tel: (356) 21556153. Open: daily 9am–5pm. Admission charge.*

Old Prison

This was used from the mid-16th century to 1904 and retains interesting historical graffiti carved by the inmates. *Citadel. Tel: (356) 21565988. Open: daily 9am–5pm. Admission charge.*

Wine tasting

At No 4 Triq il-Fosos (Fosse Street), close to the cathedral, stop to taste Ricardo Zammit's home-made wines.

These are served with Gozitan bread, tomatoes and cheese. Apart from wine you can also buy Gozitan honey, pottery, lace and other local crafts.

It-Tokk (Pjazza Indipendenza)

It-Tokk means 'the meeting place', and for centuries this tree-lined square has been the hub of town life in Victoria. Every weekday morning stalls are laid out with fish and fruit, linen and knitwear, rolls of fabric and T-shirts. Around the square, shops sell chunky jumpers and bars serve potent Gozitan wine. Within the square is a bronze statue of Christ, commemorating the Gozitan servicemen and civilians killed in World War II. Bordering the square is the recently restored 18th-century St James' Church, and the semi-circular Banca Giuratale, built in 1733 by Grand Master de Vilhena, and now used as the local council offices.

Well worth exploring are the medieval alleyways behind the square in the old part of the town. The houses have some interesting architectural features, and the tiny shops and bars here provide plenty of local colour.

St George's Basilica

The solemn, majestic Basilica of St George dominates its little square behind It-Tokk. Built in 1673, the church was badly damaged in the earthquake of 1693, and has been extended and embellished over the centuries. Sometimes called 'the Golden Basilica', its rich interior is profusely gilded, and the centrepiece is a dominant bronze canopy, imitating that of Bernini at St Peter's in Rome.
Pjazza San Ġorġ (St George's Square). Tel: (356) 21556377. Open: daily 8.30am–1pm & 2.30–7pm. Free admission.

Triq ir-Repubblika (Republic Street)

This was once known as Racecourse Street because horse-trotting races used to be held here and still are on main *festa* days. The finest feature of the street is the series of handsome houses and overhanging enclosed balconies, some of them beautifully carved.

On 15 August, the Feast of the Assumption (called Santa Marija locally), the street is also the venue for an agricultural show, attended by large numbers of Gozitans, Maltese and visitors. If you want to see it, be there early – before mid-morning.

DWEJRA COAST

Cliffs, caves and freaks of nature combine to make Dwejra's seascape the most spectacular on Gozo. In calm weather the deep, clear and intensely blue waters are excellent for diving, snorkelling and swimming. Here, too, you can see the oldest salt pans on Gozo, from which sea salt is still collected during the summer.

Azure Window (Tieqa Zerqa)

Thousands of years of erosion by the sea and the weather have created this monumental limestone archway at Dwejra Point. The ledge of rock forming the upper arch of the 'window' is in danger of collapsing – but geologists and others still walk across it looking for fossilised sea creatures.

Fungus Rock

The plant that once thrived on this steep-sided offshore rock was prized by the Knights for its medicinal properties – so much so that they jealously guarded the islet and made it inaccessible. The only way of reaching the virtually unscalable rock was by means of a hoist from the still-standing Qawra Tower to the top of the rock. Any unauthorised person found attempting to gain access was sentenced to death.

The plant was pulverised by mortar and pestle, mixed with a little wine and syrup, and taken as a cure for dysentery and haemorrhages.

The local name for the island – Il-Ġebla tal-Ġeneral, the General's Rock – is said to commemorate an Italian general who, while supervising the quarrying of the rock in the Middle Ages, fell off the cliffside and drowned.

The Inland Sea (Il-Qawra)

Inland from the Azure Window, this pool of aquamarine-coloured seawater is surrounded by high limestone cliffs, and linked to the sea by a narrow rock

Wind, rain and waves have combined to create the Azure Window

tunnel. It even has its own shingle beach, and when the open sea is rough (which it frequently is) this provides a sheltered, shallow spot for bathing. In calm weather, fishing boats can be hired for a trip through the tunnel and along the cliffs near the Azure Window.
Dwejra Point is 5.5km (3½ miles) west of Victoria. Bus 91.

GĦAJNSIELEM

The village at the top of the hill from Mġarr Harbour grew in the 17th century when a freshwater spring was discovered. The central piazza, Apparition Square, is so named after a shepherd had a vision of the Virgin Mary on the site. The village has one of Gozo's oldest chapels but the village's main place of worship is the parish church built in the 20th century in Gothic style.

GĦARB

On the west side of the island, Għarb is one of Gozo's prettiest and most peaceful villages. The stone balconies of its houses, many of them old and finely carved, are particularly attractive. Several British expatriates settled here, restoring the old village and its farmhouses.

The dominant feature of the village centre is the Baroque Church of the Immaculate Conception, whose concave façade, with its floral decoration and sculptures of Faith, Hope and Charity, makes a powerful impact. Two famous characters of Għarb are venerated in tiny museums:

The Inland Sea remains tranquil even when the open sea is stormy

Frenċ tal-Għarb, Gozo's best-known faith healer, and Carmela Grima, who heard the miraculous voices at Ta'Pinu (*see pp136–7*), which has now become a well-known pilgrimage centre for both Maltese and Gozitans.
3km (1¾ miles) northwest of Victoria. Buses 2 & 91.

MARSALFORN

From a seaside village frequented by a small number of prosperous Gozitans, Marsalforn has now become Gozo's largest resort. The fishing village has gradually extended along the crescent-shaped rocky bay, and these days, hotels, apartment blocks and souvenir shops are more prominent than the few fishing boats that dot the little harbour. The small shingle beach attracts the crowds, but venture to the northwest as the bays of Qbajjar and Xwieni are much quieter for swimming.

The salt pans all around here date from 1740 and are still in use, producing several tons of sea salt every year.

3.5km (2¼ miles) northeast of Victoria. Bus 21.

MĠARR

Arriving on Gozo from Malta, your first close-up view will be of Mġarr, where fishing boats and ferries lie in a harbour backed by flat-roofed houses on the hillside. After long delays a new ferry terminal opened here in 2007. Dominating the scene are the churches of Our Lady of Lourdes, on the craggy cliffs above the village, and of neighbouring Għajnsielem. Crowning the hilltop to the southwest are the walls and bastions of Fort Chambray (*see p142*).

6km (3¾ miles) southeast of Victoria. Bus 25.

NADUR

The name of the town comes from the Arabic for 'lookout point'. Clinging to a ridge 152m (500ft) above sea level, Nadur was the chief watchtower for the east coast at the time of the Knights.

The size and splendour of the 18th-century Baroque parish church, dedicated to Saints Peter and Paul, gives you some idea of the prosperity of the place. Seafaring activities made it rich and gave the locals a certain superiority over the rest of Gozo (or so

it is said). In the early 17th century, Grand Master Wignacourt used the woods and gardens that then flourished here as his private shooting domain. Few dared to trespass; the penalty for poaching was to spend three years rowing in a galley.

6km (3¾ miles) east of Victoria. Buses 42 & 43.

QALA

This quiet rural village east of Nadur has one of Gozo's few surviving (but no longer working) 19th-century windmills. To the east, where the coastline is characterised by cliffs and rocky outcrops, there are fine views across to the rocky island of Comino and the tiny isle of Cominotto beside it.

7km (4 miles) east of Victoria. Buses 42 & 43.

RAMLA BAY (IR-RAMLA)

North of Nadur, Ramla Bay has a splendid stretch of ochre sands, its green-blue waters protected by a rugged headland. Given the ease of access and the fact that it is the only sandy beach of any size on Gozo, it is crowded in summer. Beach facilities include cafés, watersports and parasols. Even so, you must be very careful: a notice on the beach warns swimmers of dangerous currents and reefs.

In the nearby Ramla Valley, the terraced fields, divided by bamboo fences, create a patchwork effect and lend an impressive backdrop to the bay.

Calypso's Cave

This is claimed by the Gozitans as the abode of Calypso, the sea nymph who enchanted Odysseus on his journey home from the Trojan War. The cave has since become blocked by boulders, and now amounts to no more than a crevice on the cliff. In the *Odyssey*, Homer describes Calypso's Cave as being surrounded by poplar and cypress trees, with a grape-laden vine at the opening. The best thing about the cave today is the breathtaking view over Ramla Valley and Bay.

Ramla Bay is 6.5km (4 miles) northeast of Victoria. Bus 42.

SAN BLAS BAY

The steep, narrow track down to this quiet little beach is almost inaccessible by car, but you can walk down and you will be well rewarded. There is no development here apart from a few boathouses, and the bay is a perfect spot for a picnic or a dip. Dividing San Blas from the pretty little bay of Daħlet Qorrot are the awesome Mistra Rocks.

8km (5 miles) east of Victoria.

SAN LAWRENZ

This is a cliff-top farming village on the far west side of the island, from where a spectacular road descends through arid

Ramla Bay, where Odysseus is believed to have halted on his way back from Troy

A formidable prickly pear hedge protects the greenery in front of Ta'Pinu Church

countryside to Dwejra Point. For many years San Lawrenz was home to British author Nicholas Monsarrat, who wrote the bestselling book *The Kappillan of Malta*. The Kempinski Hotel San Lawrenz resort, a five-star complex on the outskirts of the village, has given the village a new lease of life.

East of San Lawrenz you can buy local handicrafts at the Ta'Dbieġi Crafts Village and watch the artisans at work.
4km (2¹/₂ miles) northwest of Victoria.

SANNAT

A quiet agricultural village in southern Gozo, Sannat is one of the few places where you can still see lace being made. In the summer months you may see elderly women seated outside their doorways making delicate shawls, tablemats or lace-edged handkerchiefs. Sannat is also known for its carved stone balconies. These days the most

conspicuous are the brand-new ones, with their ornate and fanciful decoration. The focal point of this straggling village is the twin-belfried parish church, dedicated to St Margaret, and built in 1718 on the site of a smaller church.

Beyond the village the sheer cliffs of Ta'Cenc drop 180m (590ft) down to the sea. On the promontory lies the five-star Hotel Ta'Cenc – justifiably considered one of the most desirable hotels on the Maltese islands. Just one storey high and built in the local honey-coloured limestone, it blends in well with its surroundings. Not far away the cart tracks and dolmens are evidence of a prehistoric settlement.

From Sannat, a 1.5km (1-mile) walk along a country road and then a valley will bring you to the pretty little inlet of Mġarr ix-Xini (*see pp142–3*).
2km (1¹/₄ miles) south of Victoria. Bus 50.

TA'PINU

The modern neo-Romanesque sanctuary of Ta'Pinu rises majestically in isolated countryside, a centre of pilgrimage for Gozitans and Maltese. The original church was a simple 16th-century single-cell chapel, tended by a pious individual called Fillipino Gauci – or Pinu for short. In 1883 a local peasant woman called Carmela Grima heard a mysterious voice as she walked home to Għarb. She entered the chapel to pray and again heard the voice, commanding her to say three *Ave Marias*. The only friend she told this to, Francesco Portelli, also claimed to have heard the voice several times. These incidents were followed by a series of miraculous cures in the neighbourhood, and a year later Gozo escaped the plague that had struck Malta. As a result, numerous offerings were made to the chapel, and with these funds a new church was built, integrating the old chapel building. In 1932 Pope Pius XI raised Ta'Pinu to the status of a basilica.

Since the end of the 19th century the church has been a place of thanksgiving for those saved from disasters or those who were miraculously healed. In a side corridor there are paintings of shipwrecked sailors being saved, and reminders of miraculous cures. At the altar you can pick up a 'petition', listing the various favours you can request from Our Lady of Ta'Pinu (such as 'better position', 'raise in salary', 'sale of property', 'cure of alcoholism', 'Catholic boyfriend' and 'happy death'). You just need to tick the relevant box or boxes, and the petition envelope, with money enclosed, is placed in a basket beneath the altar.

Opposite the church, climbing up the Għammar Hill, is a set of 14 life-size statues in marble, representing the Stations of the Cross.
4km (2½ miles) northwest of Victoria, between Għammar and Għarb. Tel: (356) 21556187. Email: rector@tapinu.org. www.tapinu.org. Open: Mon–Sat 6.30am–12.15pm & *1.30–7pm, Sun 5.45am–12.15pm & 1.30–7pm. Buses 61 & 91.*

XAGĦRA

The huge and ornately embellished Baroque Church of Our Lady of Victories forms the focal point of this sprawling hilltop village. Every year on 8 September, the anniversary of the end of the Great Siege of Malta, the wraps come off the chandeliers, the silver and damask are displayed, and a statue of the Virgin is paraded through the streets. Like all good *festas*, it ends with a dazzling display of fireworks.

Festivities aside, the main magnet of Xagħra is the site of the Neolithic

One of several marble statues at Ta'Pinu

The Ġgantija temples are a unique and mysterious prehistoric site

Ġgantija temples, which is located on the edge of the village.

Like many Gozitan villages, Xagħra is rapidly expanding, and its new houses are conspicuous by their elaborate architectural features. The village square is the social centre, with locals, British expatriates and tourists congregating at the Oleander Restaurant for genuine Maltese home cooking.

For visitors looking for a base in the area, the four-star Cornucopia Hotel, converted from a farmhouse on the edge of the village, is a particularly desirable place to stay.
3km (1¾ miles) east of Victoria. Buses 64 & 65.

Ġgantija prehistoric temples

The setting of these prehistoric temples, affording a glorious panorama over a wide sweep of Gozo, is worth a visit in itself. Ġgantija means 'gigantic', and there is a legend that they were built by a female giant who carried the stone blocks on her head from Ta'Cenc. When you see the size of the megaliths you will understand why it was assumed that no mere mortal could possibly have moved them. The outer walls of the temples are built with colossal horizontal and upright blocks, some of them reaching a height of 7.5m (25ft) and weighing up to 50 tonnes (49 tons). The size apart, this complex of two temples, surrounded by a common outer wall, is impressive for its state of preservation. The temples date from 3600–3000 BC and rank among the finest in Malta.

The South Temple is the older of the two. On the left before you enter you will see the spherical stones which were used as rollers to transport the slabs. Just inside, on the left, is a recess, once filled with water, where worshippers washed their feet before entering the temple.

The temple interior consists of a smooth-walled limestone passage (once plastered and painted red) leading to the five apses; here you can see the remains of altars where the ritualistic slaughter of animals took place. The blocks across the central apse formed the main altar, and it was here that two stone heads, probably representing the goddess of fertility, were unearthed. They are now in the Archaeological Museum in Victoria (*see p128*). The apse to the left has libation holes hewn out of the limestone at the rear of the chamber. On the right there is a curious hole at the foot of a monolith which may have been an oracle hole. Another apse contains the so-called 'Pubic Triangle', which was once partnered by the stone phallus that is also in Victoria's Archaeological Museum.
On the edge of the village, well signposted off the road from Victoria and reached by a short walk from the car park.
Tel: (356) 21553194. Open: daily 9am–5pm. Admission charge.

Ninu's Cave

The grandfather of the present owner came across this cave in 1888 while searching for water. The cave, below the owner's house, is small, but has a forest of stalactites and stalagmites.

Triq Jannar (January St). Tel: (356) 21556863. Open: daily 8.30am–6pm. Admission charge.

Ta'Kola Windmill

Built in 1725, this is one of Gozo's few surviving windmills. The mill, now a museum, has been finely preserved.
Triq il-Mitħna (Windmill St). Tel: (356) 21560820. Open: daily 9am–5pm. Admission charge.

Xerri's Grotto

The father of the priest who owns Xerri's Grotto discovered this cave 70 years ago. It is larger (and more impressive) than Ninu's Cave. The priest will point out shapes – resembling a turtle, a turkey, a giraffe and a pair of elephant's ears.
Triq L-Għar ta'Xerri (Xerri's Grotto St). Tel: (356) 21560572. Open: summer daily 9am–6pm; winter daily 9am–4.30pm. Admission charge.

Xagħra's Ta'Kola Windmill is an elegant survivor of the many that once covered Gozo

XEWKIJA

The mighty Xewkija rotunda, along with Victoria's citadel, is the most conspicuous landmark on Gozo. The dome is one of the biggest in the world – yet, for the Gozitans, it is not quite big enough; the intention was to exceed the dimensions of the Mosta dome in Malta, which it beats in height, but not in diameter.

The church was built between 1951 and 1971, during which time services were held in the old Baroque church. On completion the older structure was pulled down. All that remains today are some relics in the Church Museum.

The huge dome of Xewkija's church, seen from the inside

The exterior of the church has been compared to the Salute in Venice; the proportions and the Baroque style are certainly reminiscent, although the external decoration is not as abundant. *3km (1¾ miles) southeast of Victoria. Pjazza San Gwann Battista (St John the Baptist's Square). Tel: (356) 21556793. Church open: 6am–noon & 3–8pm. Buses 42 & 43.*

XLENDI

The deep Xlendi Valley runs down to one of the prettiest creeks on the island. The idyllic bay and the glorious blue-green waters were for many years a haunt of artists and photographers. More recently, Xlendi has become very much a tourist resort, and the village has expanded to take in apartment blocks, hotels, holiday villas and souvenir shops. It is enormously popular, and in summer gets very crowded. Out of the holiday season it still manages to exude local character and undeniable charm.

The shingle beach, rocky shore and clear waters are good for swimming, and the caves and rugged reefs provide ideal conditions for snorkelling and scuba diving. On the cliffside a series of steps, with beautiful bay views, leads to a small secluded pool which was once so private and little known that the local nuns used to come here and bathe, assured of privacy.

Xlendi looks its best in the early morning or at dusk when the day-trippers have gone. Ideally, you should

Sunset at the popular Xlendi coastline

stay for an evening meal, for Xlendi is liberally endowed with good eating places, and the sunsets over the cliffs can be spectacular. Some of the restaurants on the seafront specialise in local fish and succulent giant prawns.

Għajn il-Kbira

The Knights' Wash House, where the local women used to do their laundry, is on the road from Victoria to Xlendi. Today, it is mostly used for car washing! Its spring waters were reputed to be the sweetest on Gozo.

Xlendi is 3km (1¾ miles) southwest of Victoria. Bus 87.

ŻEBBUĠ

Sprawling over a hilltop, Żebbuġ commands good views of the coast. From the village, a rough road zigzags down to the north coast, and its shoreline is characterised by numerous salt pans. Examples of Gozitan onyx marble, which is still quarried here, can be seen in the village church.

3km (1¾ miles) north of Victoria. Buses 90 & 91.

Walk: Gozo's southern shores

Step off the ferry at Mġarr, and within minutes you can be out over the cliffs enjoying some of Gozo's loveliest coastal and valley scenery. The total distance is 7.3km (4½ miles).

Allow 3 hours.

The walk starts behind the car park at the ferry terminal in Mġarr. Take the steps to the left of the bar by the information office and head west, along the coastal path. Some sections are quite rough, and should be attempted only by the more adventurous.

1 Tafal Cliffs

The cliff path takes you past boulder-strewn shores, salt pans and secluded coves. On the landward side, small sloping plots are sheltered by drystone walls, bamboo fences or clumps of prickly pears. Keep to the coastal path and ignore any tracks going inland. At one point you will come across a stone wall. You should scramble uphill beside the wall, until you find a gate in the wall. From here you can rejoin the path.

When the first set of salt pans comes into view, make towards the corner turret of Fort Chambray, and pick up the path just below it.

2 Fort Chambray

Fort Chambray was the last stronghold to be built by the Knights. Planned in 1723 as a fortified town, complete with streets, church, town square and governor's palace, the work was never fully completed; it was only through the private funds of a French Knight, Jacques François de Chambray, that the fortifications finally materialised some 26 years later.

Beyond here the track passes a high hedge of prickly pears, then follows a stone wall where cages for small birds are placed during the trapping season.

3 Mġarr ix-Xini

The squat, semi-derelict tower which soon comes into view guards the entrance of the calm, fjord-like inlet of Mġarr ix-Xini, said to be one of the harbours used by the Knights' galleys.

Today, it is one of Gozo's prettiest coves – ideal for a dip, a picnic or a boat trip. To reach it, cross the clover-strewn slopes and go down to the coast across more salt pans.

Follow the inlet as far as you can, along a drystone wall. On the landward side of the 'beach', scramble alongside another smaller wall, on the valley side. A flight of steps cut into the rock brings you down to the inlet. Next take the minor road on the far side of the inlet which climbs uphill, following the beautiful valley called Wied Ħanżira. The huge dome ahead is that of Xewkija church (see p140). After 2.5km (1½ miles) bear left at the junction for Sannat village.

Look out for the view of Victoria's citadel

4 Sannat

The agricultural village of Sannat is known for its lacemaking (*see p136*). Before reaching the centre, savour the view to your right of the flat-topped hills, the church domes, and the citadel of Victoria atop a hill to the north.

In Sannat turn right for the church and the road that will take you to Victoria (2km/1¼ miles). Alternatively, you can take bus 50.

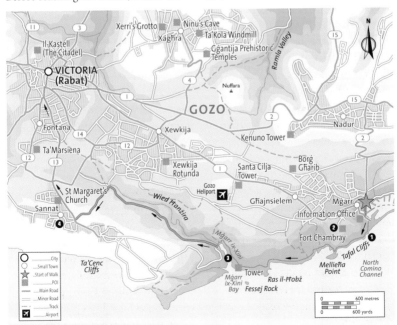

Xerri's Grotto   Ninu's Cave
Il-Kastell (The Citadel)   Xagħra   Ta'Kola Windmill
Ġgantija Prehistoric Temples
VICTORIA (Rabat)
Ramla Valley
Nuffara
GOZO
Fontana   Xewkija   Nadur
Ta'Marsiena   Kenuno Tower
Xewkija Rotunda   Santa Cilja Tower   Borġ Għarib
St Margaret's Church   Gozo Heliport
Sannat   Wied Franżira   Għajnsielem   Mġarr
Information Office
Fort Chambray
Mġarr ix-Xini
Ta'Cenc Cliffs   Tower   Mellieħa Point   North Comino Channel
Mġarr ix-Xini Bay   Ras il-Ħobż   Fessej Rock
Tafal Cliffs

○	City
○	Small Town
★	Start of Walk
■	POI
—	Main Road
=	Minor Road
⋯	Track
✈	Airport

0 — 600 metres
0 — 600 yards

Getting away from it all

Malta is so small that there are very few places, if any, which can truly be called 'undiscovered'. In summer even so-called 'secluded coves' will see a good smattering of locals and tourists, whether sunbathing on the beach, or in a boat nearby, or scuba diving among the rocks. Peace and tranquillity will only descend once the day-trippers have gone home. One way to find peace and solitude is to take to the countryside or the cliffs on foot.

Walking is not the ideal way of getting around in the heat of the summer, but out of season it's the best way of discovering the beauty spots of Malta.

More rural than Malta, Gozo offers far greater opportunity for finding peace and quiet. The ferryloads of visitors who descend daily on its shores normally concentrate on the island's highlights, leaving the isolated spots for the more independent-minded visitor.

Comino is the quietest island of the Maltese archipelago (*see pp146–7*). Officially, it has only four permanent residents, so you can truly get away!

Beaches

Most sandy beaches are packed in summer. However, on Gozo, access to the pretty San Blas Bay is sufficiently tricky to deter the majority. At Mġarr ix-Xini, on the south side of Gozo, you can swim in the transparent waters of a deep inlet (*see pp142–3*). On Malta your only hope of finding a quiet spot is by scrambling down cliffsides or walking sufficiently far from the main touristy bathing areas.

Parks and gardens

Malta has an abundance of playgrounds but a scarcity of parks and gardens. The most popular place for picnics or walks in the shade of the trees is Buskett Forest near Rabat (*see p73*). The only other public gardens of any size are those of the San Anton Palace in Attard (*see pp78–9*). These are worth visiting for their avenues of trees and flowers, but access entails a drive through the Valletta suburbs.

Jeep Safari – Gozo

For exploring the quiet corners of Gozo, access to which would seriously

---

JEEP SAFARIS

Contact: Captain Morgan Tours, Dolphin Court, Tigné Seafront, Sliema (*tel: (356) 23463333*). Reservations can also be made through hotels and travel agents.

endanger the suspension of any hired car, you can't beat the Jeep Safari.

On this trip you bump over salt pans, scale up the roughest terrain and finally reach the highest point on Gozo for a wonderful panorama of the island.

The day is a long one, starting at 7.30am if you are staying in the Sliema area. This ensures an entire day on Gozo. The ferry crossing takes 20 to 25 minutes, and there is no stopping at the busy harbour of Mġarr. You head straight for quiet countryside around Qala, taking rough tracks through fields, and admiring the views across clumps of prickly pears to the island of Comino.

On the north of the island you drive along valleys of bamboo and pine, and stop for a dip at a tiny secluded cove or the sweeping sands of Ramla Bay.

Near Marsalforn (a tourist resort which you bypass) the jeeps head for the salt pans, and drive along the sandstone rocks, skirting shimmering blue seas.

Lunch is thoroughly Gozitan, well away from the crowds, and washed down with plenty of potent local wine. Afternoons are spent exploring the fascinating west coast, where there is time to swim in the shallow waters of the Inland Sea, watch the fishermen, or merely sit and admire the beautiful seascape. The last port of call is the pretty harbour of Xlendi. Then it's back to the ferry and – after a day on peaceful, rural Gozo – the comparatively cosmopolitan atmosphere of Malta.

Getting away from it all

The peaceful and picturesque San Anton Gardens

The tiny island of Comino is a popular resort for outdoor enthusiasts

Comino

Lying between Malta and Gozo, Comino is the smallest inhabited island of the Maltese archipelago. There are no cars, no high-rise buildings, no hunters – just one hotel, a tiny hamlet, a disused cemetery and a small chapel where Mass is celebrated once a week. The only vehicles on the island are the Comino Hotel's minibus and a truck for transporting goods.

The permanent population of the island amounts to the grand total of four. In summer, however, the numbers are swollen by the staff who work in the hotel, most of them commuting from Gozo, and the visitors who come on cruisers to the Blue Lagoon, or stay for the day at the four-star Comino Hotel.

The island itself is just a bare rock with the odd patch of *maquis*

vegetation, along with a few mimosas and pines. The name Comino comes from the herbal plant cumin, which used to grow here in abundance. The island has now been made into a bird sanctuary, and the cliffs are home to small colonies of breeding seabirds.

Comino has three little sandy beaches and is surrounded by glorious ultramarine waters. Its caves and creeks are ideal for swimming, snorkelling and diving. The iridescent waters of the Blue Lagoon, which lies between Comino and the rocky islet of Cominotto, are irresistible, especially if you get here early in the day, before the cruisers and yachts arrive from Malta.

The focal point of the island is the **Comino Hotel**, which also owns the nearby bungalows. The two ferries that transport passengers from Malta and Gozo to Comino also belong to the hotel, and many of the visitors who use them have lunch at the hotel and take out day-membership for the use of the sporting facilities. So long as there are not too many other visitors with the same idea, the Comino Hotel makes a good base, located in an exotic spot with a beautiful pool right by the sea. There is a delightful sandy beach nearby, and a host of watersports facilities: sailing, windsurfing, water-skiing, snorkelling, boat trips, a diving school, canoes and paddle boats. There are also eight tennis courts, with lessons available. Those who prefer their own company can take a picnic lunch, and swim from one of the secluded spots off the rocks of the island.

In winter the hotel closes down, and your only way across to Comino is by organised boat tour, or independent water taxi. Comino is a good spot for a quiet walk at this time of year, but remember to go equipped with food and drink. The best viewpoint is the Comino Tower, built in 1618 by Grand Master Wignacourt to protect the Gozo Channel from marauders. The public are allowed access to the tower, but there are no parapets at the top. The monument is currently undergoing much-needed restoration.

Apart from the derelict isolation hospital nearby, the only other landmark (hotels apart) is the former piggery, set up to restock farms on Malta after a dreadful outbreak of African swine fever in 1980.

In season, boats depart for Comino from Ċirkewwa on Malta four times a day from 7.30am to 6.30pm. The trip takes about 25 minutes. There is also a regular seasonal service from Gozo. Timing and ticket details are available from Comino Hotel, Island of Comino. Tel: (356) 21529821.
www.cominohotel.com.
Open: Apr–end Oct.

The translucent water of Comino is irresistible

Flora and fauna

Although Malta is essentially barren, it begins to come to life with the autumn rains. The dust is washed away, and by Christmas the terraced fields are green with crops and the citrus groves are laden with fruit. The early spring, lasting until April, sees a succession of wild flowers and herbs. Sprouting from the stony soil, or seemingly solid rock, are several varieties of narcissus, iris, gladioli and marigold. Red and yellow poppies grow wild, and the blossom of rock roses dots the hillsides. In towns, pink- and white-flowered oleander trees line the avenues, while bougainvillea adds a dash of red or purple to the white walls of the villas and holiday homes.

All year round you will stumble across the very rampant Malta knapweed with its pale yellow flowers. Equally familiar is the fruit-bearing prickly pear cactus, seen growing wild by drystone walls, or as hedges to provide protection for the crops.

Very few wild animals inhabit the islands. Wild rabbits live on St Paul's Islands, and the occasional reptile may be seen, such as the chameleon, or the rare Algerian whip snake. More common are the Moorish and Turkish geckos, which were introduced to Malta over 100 years ago, and now live inside houses, helping to keep irritating insects at bay.

Malta's bird population has been drastically reduced by hunters and trappers. The national bird is the blue rock thrush, which is prized for its mellow song; it is therefore frequently trapped or robbed of its eggs. Seabirds, including yellow-legged gulls, storm petrels and shearwaters, breed on the sea cliffs around the islands.

The best time for birdwatchers to enjoy the islands' birdlife is in spring and autumn, when migratory birds stop off on their journey between Europe and North Africa for resting and refuelling on Malta's wetlands.

Rolling acres of fragrant flower-filled fields

Shopping

Malta has numerous outlets for traditional crafts, food and jewellery that have been open for decades, particularly in the backstreets of Valletta. The country has also seen a growth in big-name department stores and fashion shops trading in international brands such as Marks & Spencer, Benetton and Next.

Now the country is into the next stage of retail therapy with the emergence of shopping malls. Valletta has the Embassy complex, while St Julian's has Bay Street. The Plaza Shopping Centre in Sliema and the Duke Shopping Mall in Victoria, Gozo, are popular with local shoppers.

All these look quite modest affairs compared with the latest palace of retail trade in The Point shopping mall in Sliema, where familiar names like Debenham's, Nike, Lacoste, Esprit and M&S have all taken space in what has become Malta's first international standard shopping mall.

WHAT TO BUY
Brass and iron
Replica brass dolphin door-knockers, as seen in Mdina and other old quarters, are favourite souvenirs. Wrought ironwork is a local tradition, and items range from candlesticks to an entire suit of armour.

Ceramics
Local pottery is not as varied as you might expect from a Mediterranean island. The styles are mainly rustic, in browns and blues. Reasonably priced are the ceramic and sculpture 'seconds' sold at the Craft Centre in Ta'Qali.

Glass
Maltese and Gozitan glassware is stylish, beautifully coloured and reasonably priced.
Gozo Glass *Għarb, Gozo. Tel: (356) 21561974. Email: info@gozoglass.com. www.gozoglass.com*
Mdina Glass *Ta'Qali Craft Centre. Tel: (356) 21415786. Email: info@ mdinaglass.net. www.mdinaglass.net*

Jewellery
The Maltese have been making jewellery for centuries, and the island is full of silversmiths and goldsmiths. The streets of Valletta are the best place to shop.

Textiles

Most of the authentic handmade items you will see are made on Gozo. Beware, however, of imitation lace. Equally abundant are woollen cardigans and sweaters.

Malta Weave is an especially hard-wearing cloth that is used for making dresses, skirts, tablecloths and bedspreads. You can watch weaving displays.

WHERE TO BUY
Craft centres

Generally speaking, the best places to buy local handicrafts are the craft centres on Malta and on Gozo.

Ta'Qali Craft Centre, Ta'Qali

Authentic Maltese crafts are displayed on the site of a World War II aerodrome. Here you can watch silversmiths, glass-blowers, potters, ironsmiths, stonecarvers, lacemakers and jewellers.

A visit to the village features on day tours of the island, but it is more satisfying to go independently and browse (and buy) at your own leisure.
For full details, see pp82–3.

Ta'Dbieġi Crafts Village

This is Gozo's version of the Ta'Qali Craft Centre, displaying and selling local crafts. The emphasis is on lacemaking and weaving.
On the road between San Lawrenz and Għarb, Gozo. Tel: (356) 21561482. Open: daily 8.30am–6.45pm.

Gozo Citadel Crafts Centre

Arts and crafts purchased by private Maltese and Gozitan firms, located in what used to be the old Gozo prison. *Gozo citadel (near the cathedral).*

Street markets

Valletta's **flea market** is held on Sunday mornings near City Gate. There are also weekday markets in Merchants' Street, Valletta, in Rabat and in Marsaxlokk (*see pp100–101*); and there is a market during the week in Victoria on Gozo. For local colour nothing beats the Sunday fish market at Marsaxlokk, where the island's top chefs get the catch of the day.

Colourful Mdina glassware comes in all shapes and sizes

Entertainment

Traditionally, nightlife in the capital has tended to be very low-key, amounting to no more than a drink or two in a bar, or an evening trot in a horse-drawn karrozzin *round the city's floodlit ramparts. The evening scene has recently been enlivened by the Valletta Waterfront with its harbour-view bars, brasseries, diners and live concerts in summer. But the real action on Malta is to be found well out of the capital, in the resorts to the northwest.*

Those seeking the bright lights should head to the small area of St Julian's known as Paceville. Here you will find scores of discos, pubs and late-night bars. St Julian's is also home to one of Malta's four casinos.

Beyond the headland St George's Bay has a growing number of fashionable discos. Bars with live music and the occasional disco can be found in Sliema, and in the St Paul's area, around Buġibba and Qawra.

Hotel entertainment takes the form of folk nights, cabarets and possibly discos. These events are normally open to non-residents.

On the cultural side, Malta has several English-language theatres and cinemas. The delightful Teatru Manoel (*see p155*) puts on ballet, opera and concert performances, in addition to plays. St James Cavalier in Valletta's city walls has a small theatre and a cinema. One of the most important cultural events in the Maltese calendar is the Malta Arts Festival (*see p25*).

What's on

The Malta Tourism Authority (*see* Tourist offices, *p188*) publishes a calendar of annual events. Local newspapers have listings of cinemas, theatres and various other events.

Casinos

Malta has four casinos, offering classic table games and slot machines. Each has a restaurant and bars, and free transport can be arranged from hotels. Proof of ID is required for temporary membership. In all casinos the dress code is smart casual and after 8pm shorts, sleeveless shirts and tracksuits are not allowed. The minimum age is 18 for visitors to Malta and 25 for residents.

Casino di Venezia

Captain's Palace, Vittoriosa Waterfront. Tel: (356) 21805580. Email: reception@casinodivenezia.com.mt. www.casinodivenezia.com.mt. Open: Mon–Thur 2pm–2am, Fri–Sun noon–4am.

Dragonara Casino

Dragonara Palace, St Julian's.

Tel: (356) 21382362. www.
dragonaracasino.com. Open: Jun–Sept 24
hours; Oct–Jun Mon–Thur 10am–6am,
Fri–Sun 24 hours.

Oracle Casino
Qawra Seafront, St Paul's Bay. Tel:
(356) 21570057. www.oraclecasino.com.
Open: daily from 10am.

Portomaso Casino
St Julian's. Tel: (356) 21383777. www.
portomasocasino.com. Open: Sun–Thur
10am–5am, Fri–Sat 10am–6am.

Cinema

The **Eden Cinemas** in St George's Bay
(tel: (356) 23710400) has 17 screens
showing the latest releases and
blockbusters in English.

The **Citadel Cinema** on Castle Hill
Street, Victoria (tel: (356) 21559955),
is Gozo's main venue.

Concerts

The National Orchestra performs at the
Teatru Manoel (see p155). Classical
concerts are also held from time to time
in **St John's Co-Cathedral** in Valletta
(see pp34–7).

In summer there are occasional
concerts in the **San Anton Gardens**
in Attard (see p79) and **Buskett Forest**
near Rabat (see p73). The **Malta Jazz
Festival** (see p25) takes place in the
Grand Harbour, Valletta.

Concerts, vocal recitals, choral and
ballet presentations are organised by
the Malta Cultural Institute at the
Mediterranean Conference Centre
from January to June, and from
October to December.

The **International Choir Festival**,
held at the conference centre in
November, includes performances by
some of the leading choirs from all over
the world.

Clubs and bars
Axis
The largest disco club in Paceville
with a high-tech laser show. **Matrix**
and **Styx** are dance clubs within the
Axis complex.
Triq San Ġorġ (St George's Rd),
St Julian's. Tel: (356) 21358078.
www.fuego.com.mt. Open: daily
7pm–4am. Admission charge.

The Oracle Casino on the Promenade in St Paul's Bay

Caesar's

Popular bar in the heart of the Buġibba resort.
Bay Square, Buġibba.
Tel: (356) 21571034.
Open: daily, as a bar in daylight and disco later.

Club Numero Uno

Open-air disco near Ta'Qali Craft Centre, open Saturday night playing commercial music and Sunday night for progressive house.
Ta'Qali Craft Village, Rabat.
Tel: (356) 21358078.
www.clubnumerouno.com.
Open: Jun–Sept.

Fuego Bar

Salsa bar with DJs from South America.
Triq Sontu Wistin, St George's Bay.
Tel: (356) 21386746.
www.fuego.com.mt. Open: daily from 10.30pm.

Gianpula

Malta's largest open-air disco and techno dance club. Hosts international DJs and festival events.
Limits of Rabat.
Tel: (356) 21450238.
www.gianpula.com.
Open: Fri & Sat nights.

Havana Club

The biggest Soul, R&B and Hip-Hop club in Malta,

Dancing and drinking in one of Malta's nightclubs

located at the top of St Rita's Steps in Paceville.
Tel: (356) 21374500.
www.havanamalta.com.
Open: daily in summer.

La Grotta Disco

This is a unique disco in a cave under the street. The most attractive of all the discos on the islands.
Triq Xlendi (Xlendi Rd), Xlendi, Gozo. Tel: (356) 21551149. Open: summer daily from 9pm.
Admission charge.

Plush Lounge

Terrace with comfortable seating for watching the crowds drift by. Inside is the longest bar in town, a dance floor and a VIP area.
St George's Rd, Paceville.
Tel: (356) 27384300.
www.plush-lounge.com

Twenty Two

Cocktail bar on level 22 of the Portomaso

Business Tower, in St Julian's. A sophisticated and stylish place to meet and relax.
Tel: (356) 23102222.
www.22.com.mt

Military re-enactments

Fort St Elmo (*see p52*) is the setting of the **In Guardia**, a 40-minute re-enactment of a military parade of the Knights of St John, with period costumes and full pageantry. The event takes place on specific Sundays, at 11am. Tickets are available from tourist offices or at the entrance to the fort. (*For further information, tel: (356) 22915000.*) **Alarme!** re-creates a skirmish between Maltese and French troops in 1798. Staged at Fort St Elmo on the third Sunday of

the month Feb–Jun & Oct–Nov at 11am.
Knights Spectacular 1565 is a lively dinner show focusing on the siege.
Montekristo Estates, Hal Farrug (near Siġġiewi).
www.malta1565.com

Night excursion
Captain Morgan's Fernandes Sunset Cruise
The trip takes tourists to St Paul's Island for a swim, buffet with plenty of rum punch, and optional dancing.
Captain Morgan Tours. Tel: (356) 23463333. www.captainmorgan.com.mt. Boats depart from Sliema Marina Jun–Oct Fri & Sun.

Theatre, ballet and opera
Teatru Manoel
Valletta's delightful Teatru Manoel is Malta's main venue for music, dance and drama. Performances take place all year round, but the main season lasts from October to May. The theatre alone is worth a visit (*see pp46–7*). Both local and foreign artists perform at the theatre,

and there are occasional visits from world-famous pianists, singers and actors. Plays are regularly performed in English. One of the regular highlights is the Christmas pantomime.
St James Cavalier
The arts centre just inside the city walls of Valletta has a small theatre in the round for drama and fringe theatre productions and a cinema for art-house films.
Pjazza Kastilja, Valletta. Tel: (356) 21223200. Email: info@sjcav.org. www.sjcav.org
Astra Theatre
Built in the 1960s as a theatre, the Astra has been used principally as an opera house for the last 15 years. For financial reasons it also doubles as a cinema.
Triq ir-Repubblika (Republic St), Victoria. Tel: (356) 21556256.
Aurora Opera House
This rival to the Astra is renowned for opera and also stages plays and acts as a cinema.
Centru Parrokjali Katidral, Triq ir-

Repubblika (Republic St), Victoria. Tel: (356) 21562974. www.leone.org.mt

Walk-through experience
Relive the Great Siege of Malta (*see pp16–17*) in an action-packed 3-D experience. A souvenir shop, La Valette Vaults, sells mementos.
Great Siege Events Museum, Café Premiere Complex, Misrah ir-Repubblika (Republic Square), Valletta. Tel: (356) 21237574. http://greatsiege.com.mt. Open: daily 10am–5pm.

Historical military parade

Children

The Maltese love children and welcome them with the warmth and enthusiasm you might expect of a Mediterranean people. Malta may not be the obvious choice for a bucket-and-spade holiday (sandy beaches are scarce), nor are there many theme parks. The island does, however, offer dozens of playgrounds, an abundance of cafés serving sausages and chips, and sunshine for most of the year, in addition to its sparkling blue waters for swimming and boat trips.

Boat trips and cruises

The traditional harbour cruise (*see pp48–9*) takes in historical forts, battlements and creeks, and is fun for all ages. Or you can take boat tours around Malta or Gozo, cruising alongside caves, grottoes and salt pans, and stopping for a dip and buffet lunch in one of the bays. The day trip to Gozo or Comino takes in a dip in the glorious Blue Lagoon, with its clear, shallow waters and the sandy seabed.

The Underwater Safari boat trips from Sliema and Buġibba provide plenty of fun as you peer through underwater windows at fishes, marine flora and shipwrecks (*see p118*). *These trips are organised by Captain Morgan Cruises, Hera Cruises and Alliance Cruises. Tickets for tours can be bought in advance from hotels, travel agents and numerous outlets throughout the islands. Pick-ups can normally be arranged from the hotels.*

Children's attractions

Jokers Family Fun

With funfair games, carousel rides, video games and a soft-play area, this has everything to keep energetic kids occupied.
Level 2, Bay Street Complex, St George's Bay, St Julian's. Tel: (356) 23722300. www.jokersfamilyfun.com

Playmobil Fun Park

Toy factory (visits can be arranged on request) and play area.
HF80, Industrial Estate, Hal Far. Tel: (356) 22242445. Open: daily 10am–6pm. Free admission. Bus 13 from Valletta.

Popeye Village

Children naturally enjoy the film set of *Popeye* (*see p115*) at Anchor Bay and the adjoining play park.

Splash and Fun Park/Mediterraneo Marine Park

You can't miss this huge complex on a quiet stretch of coastline, providing a leisure park and dolphin and sea lion shows (*see p119*).

Hotels and self-catering

The few hotels with sandy beaches (among them Ramla Bay, Paradise Bay, Radisson Blu Golden Sands) provide children's facilities, but are far from the main centres. Many of the large hotels in St Julian's Bay or Buġibba also offer a range of children's facilities, including swimming pools.

Museums and culture

There are very few museums geared to children. For nature lovers the **Natural History Museum** in Mdina (*see pp69–70*) has displays of local birds, fish, mammals and shells. Very small children should not visit the neighbouring **Mdina Dungeons** (*see p69*), although older children will love the gruesome scenes of death and torture. There is a **Toy Museum** in Republic Street, Valletta, and another museum of toys in Xagħra on Gozo. The multivision shows – such as the

Malta Experience (*see pp45–6*), the **Mdina Experience** (*p69*) and **Gozo 360°** (*p130*) – are lively and spectacular enough for children of around seven and upwards to enjoy.

Swimming and sports

For children who are able to swim there are excellent bathing facilities. Rowing boats and pedalos can be hired from most of the main bays. Tuition is available in waterskiing and windsurfing, and from Golden Bay and Mellieħa Bay children can enjoy a high-speed trip on an inflatable 'sea-sausage'. Day or weekly membership is available at beach clubs – which provide watersports and other facilities – such as **Reef Club** at Dragonara Peninsula and **Lido San Gorg**, St George's Bay.

For older groups, **Paceville**, St Julian's, provides a bowling centre and a cluster of lively clubs.

The Toy Museum in Valletta will keep children amused

Sport and leisure

Sports enthusiasts are spoilt for choice on Malta. The climate and clear waters make for excellent watersports and some of the best diving in the Mediterranean. Many large hotels have their own sporting or recreational facilities, and, if not, there are several sports clubs to choose from, including the Marsa Sports and Country Club, the island's principal sporting venue.

Marsa Sports and Country Club

This huge sporting complex has sufficient facilities to keep you active for days. Affordable membership is available on a daily or weekly basis. Facilities include an 18-hole golf course, 17 hard tennis courts, 5 squash courts, an 18-hole mini-golf course, a cricket pitch and billiards tables. In addition, there is a fitness centre and, in season, a large open-air swimming pool. In the vicinity of the club there are polo grounds, a horse-racing track, football and rugby pitches, and an athletics track.

4km (2¹/₂ miles) south of Valletta, on the outskirts of Marsa. Tel: (356) 21233851. www.marsasportsclub.com

LAND SPORTS
Athletics

The Malta Marathon is an established event, held in late February. The route is 42km (26 miles) from Rabat to Sliema. A half-marathon is run concurrently. The Malta Amateur Athletic Association organises track and field events, which culminate in the athletics championships held in May at the Marsa Stadium.

Bowling

The **Eden Super Bowl** (*St George's Bay, St Julian's; tel: (356) 23710777; www.edenleisure.com*) has 20 lanes for tenpin bowling, with computerised scoring. The Malta Tenpin Bowling Association organises a variety of tournaments and championships here. The Maltese *bocci* (akin to the French pétanque) is very popular at village level.

Football

Football is extremely popular in Malta, and there are countless teams on the islands. The regular football season is from September to May. Malta competes at an international level, and the main venue is the National Stadium at Ta'Qali. This is the headquarters of the local Football Association (*tel: (356) 21222697. www.mfa.com.mt*).

Golf

Malta has only one golf course (18-hole) at the **Royal Malta Golf Club** at the Marsa Sports and Country Club (*tel: (356) 21227019; see p158*). Visitors can join on a daily or weekly basis, and lessons are available from the resident professional. Reservations are recommended. Golf attire is compulsory.

Horse racing

After football this is Malta's top spectator sport, and on Sunday afternoons from October to May, the Marsa Racecourse draws large crowds. Programmes normally consist of seven or eight trotting races and one flat race. For the times of races, look in the local papers. For info, contact:

Malta Racing Club
Tel: (356) 21222222.
www.maltaracingclub.com

Horse riding

Riding and lessons are available at the following schools:

Bidnija Horse Riding School
John Mary House, Triq il-Bdiewa, Bidnija. Tel: (356) 21414010.
www.bidnijahorseriding.com

Darmanin Equestrian Enterprises
15/1 Rosary Flats, St Vincent St, Hamrun. Tel: (356) 21238507. Stables in Marsa. Tel: (356) 21227035.
www.darmaninequestrian.com

Golden Bay Horse Riding School
Għajn Tuffieħa. Tel: (356) 21573360.
www.goldenbayhorseriding.com

Putting for a birdie at Royal Malta Golf Club

Tennis and squash

Some hotels have their own courts, and there are excellent facilities for tennis and squash players at the Marsa Sports and Country Club (*see p158*) and at the **Vittoriosa Lawn Tennis Club** (*Corradino Heights, Paola; tel: (356) 21696978; www.vltc.com.mt*).

Courts are also available at **Union Club Malta** (*Tigné St, Sliema; tel: (356) 21332011*).

Walking

Malta Nature Tours organises guided country walks for small groups.
www.maltanaturetours.com

WATERSPORTS
Diving

Malta and Gozo are ideal for diving (*see pp162–3*) and the costs are reasonable by European standards.

A full range of PADI (Professional Association of Diving Instructors) and BSAC (British Sub-Aqua Club) courses is offered, as well as taster sessions for the total beginner.

Diving takes place either from the shore or from boats. For any diving course you need a medical certificate of physical fitness. This can be arranged locally for a fee (though sometimes the fee will already be included in the price of a course).

All necessary equipment can be hired on the spot. Any experienced diver wishing to dive independently of a diving school must obtain a Malta Government Dive Permit, or present a certificate to the authorities equivalent to at least the PADI advanced or the CMAS (Confédération Mondiale des Activités Subaquatiques) two-star certificate. The following are reliable licensed diving schools:

Atlantis Diving Centre
Qolla St, Marsalforn.
Tel: (356) 21554685.
www.atlantisgozo.com

Calypso Diving Centre
Marsalforn Bay.
Tel: (356) 21561757.
www.calypsodivers.com

Diveshack
14a Qui-Si-Sana Place, Sliema.
Tel: (356) 21338558.
www.divemalta.com

Divewise Services
Dragonara Complex, St Julian's.
Tel: (356) 21336441.
www.divewise.com.mt

Maltaqua
Triton Court, Triq il-Mosta (Mosta Rd), St Paul's Bay.
Tel: (356) 21571873. www.maltaqua.com

Subway Scuba Diving
Vista Complex, Pioneer Rd, Buġibba.
Tel: (356) 21572997.
www.subwayscuba.com

Fishing

No fishing licence is required, and fishing is permitted from the rocks anywhere around the islands. It is possible to go out to sea if you arrange it with a local fisherman, but you are likely to pay a great deal for the privilege. Ask at the village of Marsaxlokk and be prepared to bargain.

Sailing and yachting

Regattas are held from March to November, many of them starting from the Royal Malta Yacht Club. The principal events are the Comino Regatta in June, the Malta to Syracuse (Sicily) keelboat race in July and the Middle Sea Race in October.

Malta has exceptionally good boating facilities. The 247-berth at Grand Harbour Marina has increased the capacity of Malta's yacht marinas to over 1,500. The main yachting centre focuses on Msida Marina and Whitehall Quay, both on Msida Creek, which together provide around 700 berths. The Mġarr Marina on Gozo now accommodates 150 berths. For information on chartering yachts and on international competitions:

The Royal Malta Yacht Club

Ta'Xbiex Seafront, Ta'Xbiex.
Tel: (356) 21333109. Email:
info@rmyc.org. www.rmyc.org

The Malta Sailing School offers courses in dinghies and keelboats for beginners and experienced sailors.

Snorkelling

The clear Maltese waters are excellent for snorkelling. Equipment can be bought or hired locally.

Water polo

The Maltese are mad about water polo, and special pools have been constructed in some of the main centres. The national pitch is at Tal-Qroqq in Msida.

Waterskiing

Facilities are available on the main beaches. The most popular are to be found at Malta's Mellieħa Bay and Golden Bay. Waterskiing trips and tuition are available from:
Paradise Diving, *Paradise Bay Hotel, Ċirkewwa. Tel: (356) 21524363. www.paradisediving.com*

Windsurfing

Windsurfing boards can be hired at the main beaches in Malta. Mellieħa is particularly good.

The Sicily–Malta Windsurfing Race, held in May, and the International Open Class Boardsailing Championships, held in September and October, both attract competitors at international level.

Fishing is possible all year round in Malta

Plumbing the depths

The Maltese islands have crystal-clear warm waters, which make them a natural diving destination at any time of the year. The underwater scenery is made even more exciting by a number of wreck dive sites around the islands.

You are unlikely to encounter exotic tropical fish in the Mediterranean, but you will see grouper, amberjack, bream, squid and octopus in the caves and grottoes of the coastline. In winter many species of fish move closer to the shore and you get a better chance to observe and photograph them.

Malta is a great place for your first scuba diving adventure or for exploration and training if you already have some experience. There are many dive centres around Malta with all the equipment you will need and qualified instructors. Several dive centres are based in resort hotels.

Some of the best dive sites are on Gozo and Comino and many are best reached from a boat. Some centres organise night dives.

Dive sites
Ċirkewwa

A good spot for beginners. There is a submerged Madonna statue and a rock formation called 'The Arch'. More experienced divers can explore the wreck of the tug boat *Rozi*. Dive depth: 18–30m (60–100ft).

Għar Lapsi

A south-coast dive site with a system of colourful caves, lit up with shafts of sunlight. Dive depth: up to 20m (65ft).

Valletta

A wreck dive suitable for beginners. Explore the remains of HMS *Maori*, a destroyer sunk in the harbour in 1942. Dive depth: 12–16m (40–50ft).

Wied iż-Żurrieq

A good variety of marine life including octopus and barracuda among the reefs. Dive depth: 9m (30ft).

Dwejra, Gozo

A dive for the more experienced, the Blue Hole is one of the most spectacular dive sites in the islands. You can swim under the famous Azure Window and explore a large underwater cave. Dive depth: over 20m (65ft).

Santa Maria Caves, Comino

These are shallow, interlocking caves with a lot of fish activity, reached from a boat dive. Octopus, moray eels and small fish are common sights here. Dive depth: up to 20m (65ft).

The facilities for divers are excellent on Malta, and the visibility is outstanding; the attractions include sunken wrecks and varied marine life

Food and drink

Malta has seen a great improvement in recent years in the choice of places to eat out. Beyond the proliferation of pizzerias, pasta houses and snack bars, there are occasional gourmet restaurants, and a good range of places serving fresh fish. The fish establishments can be anything from family-run seaside cafés to fully-fledged restaurants which entice you with their tanks full of live lobsters.

What to eat

Menus are almost always translated into English. The following are a few of the local dishes which you may come across if you happen to eat in restaurants serving Maltese cuisine.

Soups

Aljotta: fish soup seasoned with onions and herbs

Brodu: basic soup made from boiled beef and flavoured with celery, marrow and turnip

Kawlata: vegetable soup with added pork or Maltese sausages

Minestra: vegetable soup, similar to minestrone but thicker

Soppa tal-armla: vegetable soup served with goat's cheese

Pasta and rice

Ravjul: Maltese ravioli, stuffed with ricotta cheese

Ross fil-forn: baked rice cooked with minced beef, eggs, tomatoes and saffron

Timpana: macaroni layered with meat,

vegetables, cheese and eggs, baked in pastry

Vegetables

Locally grown vegetables are often served with a stuffing made of minced meat, onions, parsley, olives, bread-crumbs, herbs and tomato purée.

Brungiel: stuffed aubergines

Kapunata: aubergines, tomatoes, green peppers and garlic

Qaqoċċ mimli: stuffed globe artichokes

Qara'bali mimli: stuffed marrow

Fish

Fresh fish is expensive and not always available, especially in winter. 'Fresh' on a menu may merely mean that the fish was frozen as soon as it was caught.

Accola: amberjack

Awwija: lobster

Calamari: squid (stuffed, fried or braised)

Cerna: grouper

Clamar: squid

Dott: stone bass
Fanfru: pilot fish (a member of the mackerel family)
Gamblu: prawn
Granċ: crab
Lampuka: dorado
Merluzzo: red mullet
Pagell: red bream
Pagru: sea bream
Pixxispad: swordfish
Qarnita: octopus
San Pietro: John Dory
Sargu: white bream
Skorfna: rock fish
Spnotta: sea bass
Tamal: mussels
Tunnagg: tuna

Meat
Braġioli: slices of beef rolled round a mixture of minced meat, olives, egg, bacon, breadcrumbs and parsley
Fenek biz-zalza: rabbit stew, made with onions, herbs and wine
Torta tal-fenek: rabbit pie

Cheese
Ġbejna is sheep's milk cheese, served either fresh, half-dried or peppered. A speciality of Gozo, this comes in small rounds, and is excellent with the local bread and tomatoes.

Bread
Maltese bread (*hobz*) is very crusty on the outside and soft inside. According to a national newspaper survey, the average daily consumption is a kilo (2lb) of bread per person! If you taste the real thing, made by traditional methods (as still used in Qormi), you will understand why.

What to drink
Since joining the EU, Malta has enjoyed tax-free imported wines. Prices have dropped and a large number of wine bars have appeared on the island. As for Maltese wine, the EU is funding new vineyards and the quality of locally produced wine has seen a marked improvement over recent years. The main wineries are **Delicata**, **Marsovin**, **Meridiana** and the newcomers, **Camilleri** and **Montekristo** (*see pp76–7*). Some Maltese wine is made from grapes imported from Italy and pressed in Malta.

Wine made from grapes grown in Malta will carry the DOK or IGT marks on their labels, in line with European standards.

Among the beers available in Malta, **Cisk** and **Hopleaf** are popular brands of lager. For a *digestif* after dinner, a Maltese liqueur called **Bajtra** is a sweet concoction made from the prickly pear, and **Limuncell** is a liqueur made from lemons grown on Gozo.

Maltese bread is well worth sampling

Maltese regional cuisine

High standards of cuisine were introduced to Malta by the Knights. Food came high on the list of priorities for this supposedly monastic and frugal order. To serve their tastes, chefs were shipped in from abroad, wine flowed in from France and ice was imported from the snowy peak of Mount Etna, on the island of Sicily.

Foreign influences still play a major role in Maltese cuisine. The island's close proximity to Italy has inevitably determined its favourite dish of pasta; the British left their mark in the form of roast beef, apple pie and, of course, fish and chips.

The real local dishes, however, have the unmistakable stamp of the Mediterranean. Essential ingredients are the local herbs and vegetables, such as sun-ripened tomatoes, green peppers, marrows and artichokes. Made into bulky Maltese soups, and eaten with the local crusty bread, these make a more than adequate meal. Fish is abundant and comes steamed, braised or grilled. Choose from sea bream, swordfish, grouper, tuna, pilot fish, amberjack, prawns, lobsters – and many more. Autumn brings the *lampuka*, a fish that breeds near the Nile Delta and swarms around the Maltese coast in September and October. Its somewhat enigmatic taste has been compared to cod, mackerel and whitebait! It is perhaps best tasted in the form of lampuka pie, cooked with tomatoes, onions, parsley, peas and cauliflower, then encased in light and crispy pastry.

Among the few regional meat dishes of Malta is *braġioli*, similar to beef olives, made with thin slices of beef wrapped round a minced pork,

Traditional Maltese food ranges from tasty parcels of pastry filled with cheese to…

...fresh seafood and rabbit stew

egg and bacon stuffing. Done well, it is absolutely delicious.

A favourite and long-established Maltese dish is rabbit. This is served in a variety of forms, which you can taste by going out for a traditional *fenkata* (or 'rabbit evening'). This starts with spaghetti in rabbit sauce, followed by fried rabbit or rabbit stew (complete with liver and kidneys); the meal ends with nuts and figs. Ideally, you should experience this in a basic country bar, full of villagers, and wash it down with lots of local wine. The village of Mġarr on Malta is the place to try it.

Where to eat

The majority of Malta's restaurants serve Italian food, and range from basic pasta houses to four-star restaurants. In addition, there are pubs and cafés serving typical British fare, a growing number of ethnic restaurants (particularly in St Julian's), a handful of top-notch gourmet restaurants, wine bars offering cold cuts and cheeses, and a multitude of fast-food outlets. Simple village bars can produce some surprisingly wholesome meals at rock-bottom prices. Most Maltese cuisine is meat- or fish-based, and the best bets for vegetarians are pasta, salads and the delicious local cheeses.

Most restaurants close for one day a week, and some shut in midwinter. Lunch is served from noon to about 3pm. Evening meals are served from 6pm or 7pm to about 10.30pm.

Prices

In the following list of recommended

Bars are great places to meet friendly locals

restaurants, the price symbol indicates the approximate cost per person of a three-course meal, including half a bottle of local wine. The price for fresh fish is frequently not shown on menus, to allow for seasonal availability and fluctuating market prices. Make sure to ask before you order.

★ under €30
★★ €30–40
★★★ over €40

MALTA
Dingli
Bobbyland Restaurant ★
A great place to stop for home-made rabbit stew in garlic and a selection of salads and pasta including vegetarian options.
Panoramic Rd, Dingli Cliffs. Tel: (356) 21452895. www.bobbyland.eu

Marsaskala
Tal Familja ★★
Family-run seafood restaurant which also has a wide range of vegetarian dishes.
Triq il-Gardiel. Tel: (356) 21632161. www. talfamiljarestaurant.com

Marsaxlokk
Pisces ★–★★
Waterside fish restaurant; modern décor. Vegetarian options.

86 Xatt is-Sajjieda.
Tel: (356) 21654956.

Mdina
Palazzo Costanzo ★
The *palazzo* is 17th century, the food superior Italian-Maltese and the atmosphere romantic.
Villegaignon St.
Tel: (356) 27454625.

Bacchus ★★
Housed in two chambers built in 1657 as arsenals, the place retains its original character and the food is excellent.
1 Inguanez St.
Tel: (356) 21454981.

Ciappetti ★★
Traditional Maltese dishes with a very modern twist. Seafood specials including octopus pasta and vegetarian options. Get a table in the courtyard if you can.
5 St Agatha's Esplanade.
Tel: (356) 21459987.
Email: ciappetti@ kemmunet.net.mt

Medina ★★
International cuisine and the ambience of a lovely old house.
7 Holy Cross St.
Tel: (356) 21454004.

Vinum at Fontanella ★★
Wine bar and restaurant in the evenings, on the Mdina city walls.
1 Bastion St.
Tel: (356) 21453089.

Mellieħa
Giuseppi ★★
A restaurant and wine bar, with rustic décor and innovative cuisine. Dinner only.
25 St Helen St.
Tel: (356) 21574882.

The Arches ★★★
Malta's first 'posh' restaurant has been around for 30 years. The menu changes weekly.
113 G Borg Olivier St.
Tel: (356) 21523460.
www.thearchesmalta.com

Mġarr
Charles ★
Basic, unpretentious; a great place for rabbit.
10 Jubilee Esplanade.
Tel: (356) 21573235.

il-Barri ★★
Famous for the best-value and most tender stewed rabbit for miles. Visit the air-raid shelter in the basement.
Church Square.
Tel: (356) 21573235.

The tempting Maltese rabbit stew

Mosta

Ta'Marija ★★

Traditional Maltese cuisine and entertainment by local musicians most nights.
Constitution St.
Tel: (356) 21434444.
www.tamarija.com

Lord Nelson ★★★

Small, elegant restaurant serving exquisite nouvelle cuisine.
278 Main St.
Tel: (356) 21432590.

Rabat

Ristorante Cosmana Navarra ★★

Excellent Maltese-Italian dishes including fish.
28 St Paul's St.
Tel: (356) 21450638.

St Julian's

Piccolo Padre ★

Pizzeria with sea views in the same building as Barracuda, but less formal. Vegetarian options.
195 Main St, Balluta Bay.
Tel: (356) 21344875.

L-Ghonnella ★★

The candlelit cellars of the old Spinola Palace are the setting for this upmarket place serving contemporary Maltese cuisine.

Off St George's Rd.
Tel: (356) 21351027.
www.ghonnella.com

Peppino's Wine Bar & Restaurant ★★

The in-place for society-conscious Maltese of all ages. The ground-floor wine bar serves light meals; the upstairs restaurant has excellent à la carte Italian food.
31 St George's Rd.
Tel: (356) 21373200.
www.peppinosmalta.com

Bouzouki ★★★

Superb Greek food and a terrific view over Spinola Bay.
135 Spinola Rd.
Tel: (356) 21387127.

St Paul's Bay

Ta'Cassia ★★

Mediterranean and Maltese dishes, served in a mature garden or beside a log fire in winter. Set in an old building overlooking 17th-century salt pans on the road to St Paul's Bay.
Salina Bay.
Tel: (356) 21571435.
www.tacassia.com

Sliema

Fresco's ★

A modern restaurant serving pizza and pasta.

Wide selection of vegetarian and gluten-free options.
Tower Rd.
Tel: (356) 27344763.

L'Artist ★★

A cosy, family-run restaurant with a great atmosphere. Steak is cooked on lava stones and the fish is fresh each day. Vegetarian pasta dishes. A hidden gem.
6 Tigné St.
Tel: (356) 27200870.

Salini ★★

Dramatic setting for dinner, looking across to the Valletta skyline. International dishes including a vegetarian selection.
Tigné Point, Sliema.
Tel: (356) 20603434.
Email: info@salini.com.mt

The Kitchen ★★★

Popular with Sliema foodies, this is a smart, contemporary eatery with innovative, Mediterranean cuisine.
210 Tower Rd.
Tel: (356) 21311112.

Valletta

Chiaroscuro ★

Popular Italian-style café in the day and wine bar

bistro at night, in the heart of Valletta.
44 Strait St.
Tel: (356) 27941056.

Da Pippo ★
A small trattoria with a huge reputation. The menu changes daily and they serve especially good fresh fish.
136 Melita St.
Tel: (356) 21248029.

Scalini ★
Good meat and fish dishes at this simple and relaxed Italian place.
32 South St.
Tel: (356) 21244531.
Open: evenings only.

Bologna ★★
This unpretentious place is always packed, especially at lunchtimes.
59 Republic St.
Tel: (356) 21246149.

Rubino ★★
Julian Sammut is passionate about authentic Maltese cuisine, as testified in his bistro-like restaurant.
53 Old Bakery St.
Tel: (356) 21224656.
Open: Mon–Fri.

Fusion 4 ★★★
A fashionable new restaurant set within the old city bastions, serving outstanding fusion cuisine.
1 St John's Cavalier St.
Tel: (356) 21225255.

GOZO
Għarb
Jeffrey's ★★★
One of Gozo's most popular restaurants, housed in a charming converted farmhouse.
10 Għarb Rd.
Tel: (356) 21561006.
Open: mid-Mar–Oct.

Victoria
Ta'Rikardu ★
Delightful restaurant within the citadel, serving Gozitan cheese, salads, pasta and home-made vegetable soup. Gozo wine and glassware on sale.
Fosse St.
Tel: (356) 21555953.

Brookies ★★
Set in a converted farmhouse, this is a hugely popular restaurant.
1/2 Wied Sarra St.
Tel: (356) 21559524.

Maji ★★
A stylish contemporary restaurant and wine bar.
6 Sir Adrian Dingli St.
Tel: (356) 21550878.
www.majiwine-dine.com

Patrick's Tmun ★★★
Elegant award-winning restaurant with an extensive wine list. Four specials each day in addition to the printed seasonal menu. Booking essential.
Europe St.
Tel: (356) 21566667.
www.patrickstmun.com

Xagħra
Oleander ★
Meet the locals in this friendly restaurant looking on to the village square.
10 Victory Square.
Tel: (356) 21557230.

Xlendi
Ic-Cima ★
Excellent family-run restaurant.
St Simon St.
Tel: (356) 21558407.

Gozitan food display

Accommodation

Part of Malta's success as a holiday destination is the wide choice of accommodation on offer. While some parts of the islands look overdeveloped with cheap package-holiday complexes, newer developments have been in the luxury range of hotel spa resorts. It is also possible to get away from it all by staying in a remote but modernised farmhouse or in an apartment in a former palace, and there are good deals for every budget.

Hotels

For a small island state, Malta has an extraordinary number of luxury five-star and four-star hotels.

There are more in the three-star category, of course, and plenty of cheap and cheerful seaside properties. Some hotels offer apartments with their own kitchen facilities.

Malta has over 200 hotels and it is rare that all will be full at any time of year. Outside the peak summer season there are some huge discounts and great deals to be found.

Each hotel is inspected by the Malta Tourism Authority and the star grading is based on the facilities offered rather than style and character or price.

There are wide variations in style and service within the other star categories and three-star hotels in Malta fall well short of what you would expect. A two-star hotel in Malta is very basic indeed.

Hotels in Malta tend to be large complexes, designed as self-contained resorts with all facilities on-site

including swimming pools and restaurants.

The large luxury hotels are equipped with modern health and well-being facilities including spa, sauna, steam rooms, fitness studios and various styles of massage therapy. The Fortina Spa Resort in Sliema has four spa centres and spa baths in bedrooms.

Most hotels are on the coast, but even inland on these small islands you are never very far from the sea. The fishing villages of Malta's south coast and the Gozo resorts of Xlendi and Marsalforn are also places where you can get away from it all in small hotels and guesthouses.

The townships of Buġibba and Qawra surrounding St Paul's Bay on

Peak holiday times for the Maltese islands are between May and September, Christmas, Carnival (the weekend before Lent) and Easter. You are advised to make your reservation well in advance if you intend to visit at these times.

Malta's northeast coast now have so many large cheap hotels that they are in danger of being as overdeveloped as some parts of Spain, but they remain popular with package holidaymakers.

Prices vary enormously not only between the different grades and standards, but also according to the time of year and the demand. The global financial downturn of recent years has had a big impact on Malta with a marked drop in visitors – especially out of season – and this led many of the premium hotels to offer extraordinary discounts.

At any time of the year it is possible to get a good deal in Malta; published hotel room rates are a guide but with online booking, promotional offers and package holidays booked with major tour operators, few people ever need pay the top rate.

Guesthouses

The names of Maltese guesthouses – ranging from Fawlty Towers to The Ritz – are no indication of their real character. These are normally family-run establishments, categorised into 'standard' and 'comfort' class, with the latter being the highest category. For those who want to get to know the Maltese (and perhaps try out some genuine Maltese home-cooked cuisine), a guesthouse has obvious advantages.

Youth hostels

Malta is a member of Hostelling International and has youth hostels at Buġibba, Gżira, Sliema and at Għajnsielem near Mġarr Harbour on Gozo (for information and online booking *see www.hihostels.com*).

Self-catering accommodation

Malta has an abundance of self-catering accommodation, ranging from basic one-room studios, to large apartments in huge holiday complexes, complete with their own pools, bars, shops, gym, restaurants and evening entertainment. The vast majority of these apartments and 'aparthotels' are located in Sliema, St Julian's, Qawra and Buġibba.

In contrast to the big and anonymous apartment blocks, there are a number of more exclusive holiday villages, where accommodation is provided in bungalows, villas or low-rise apartment blocks. These establishments include facilities such as swimming pools, a restaurant and a sports centre.

Renting a converted farmhouse is becoming increasingly popular, particularly on Gozo.

Prices

Hotel prices vary enormously according to demand at different times of the year. The following star ratings are used to indicate the average cost of a double room per night in high season:

★	under €80
★★	€80–150
★★★	over €150

MALTA
Attard
Corinthia Palace ★★★
A luxury hotel at the very centre of Malta and a real alternative to the bustle of the resorts. Rooms are beautifully decorated and furnished and the spa offers a wide range of treatments.
De Paule Ave.
Tel: (356) 21440301.
www.corinthia.com

Golden Bay
Radisson Blu (SAS) Golden Sands ★★★
Top-class resort hotel built on one side of Golden Bay. Three highly rated restaurants, private beach and watersports. Children catered for, and full disabled access.
Tel: (356) 23561000.
www.islandhotels.com

Mdina
Xara Palace ★★★
The only hotel in Mdina, and some would say the best in Malta. The hotel is set in an 18th-century palace and has a fine restaurant serving Italian and French dishes. Ten rooms and seven suites.

Misrah il-Kunsill.
Tel: (356) 21450560.
www.xarapalace.com.mt

St Julian's
Alfonso Hotel ★
Comfortable, clean hotel with 28 rooms.
Triq il-Qaliet.
Tel: (356) 21350053.
www.alfonsohotel.com
Highlander Guest House ★
Studio apartments with kitchenette. Bar with food downstairs.
Triq Eija Zammit.
Tel: (356) 21376609.
Email: info@ maltahighlander.com
Hotel Euro Star ★
Basic, comfortable two-star hotel convenient for the Paceville scene.
Ball St, Paceville.
Tel: (356) 21377206.
www.eurostarmalta.com
The George ★★
New stylish hotel in the heart of the Paceville district but a calm oasis from the hustle and bustle. Eco-friendly operation including solar power, and everything possible is recycled. Indoor pool with sauna and spa, rooftop lounge.

Paceville Ave.
Tel: (356) 20111000.
www.thegeorgemalta.com
Hotel Juliani ★★
Unusual for Malta, a small boutique design hotel. Set in a converted town house, overlooking Spinola Bay, with modern amenities including free Wi-Fi and a rooftop swimming pool.
12 St George's Rd.
Tel: (356) 21388000.
www.hoteljuliani.com
Hotel Valentina ★★
Stylish family-run hotel in a quiet residential part of St Julian's but very close to the nightlife scene. Eco-friendly waste and water management. 32 rooms but expanding.
Schreiber St, Paceville.
Tel: (356) 21382232.
www.valentinahotelmalta. com
Corinthia St George's Bay ★★★
Large five-star hotel overlooking the bay.
St George's Bay.
Tel: (356) 21374114.
www.corinthia.com
Hilton Malta ★★★
Centrepiece of the fashionable Portomaso

Marina development, with an extensive range of facilities including a private beach club, dive centre, four outdoor pools, fitness centre and children's play area. Full disabled access.
Portomaso.
Tel: (356) 21383383.
www.malta.hilton.com

InterContinental Malta ★★★
Modern luxury hotel set in the heart of the Paceville district with a private beach on St George's Bay, indoor and outdoor pools, fitness centre and seven restaurants. Disabled access including three rooms adapted for wheelchair users.
St George's Bay.
Tel: (356) 21377600.
www.intercontinental.com/icmalta

Westin Dragonara Resort ★★★
Luxury hotel occupying the tip of a peninsula with breathtaking views

Most four-star hotels on Malta have a swimming pool

all around. Famous casino within the complex. Facilities include the Divewise diving centre, self-drive speedboats, seven restaurants, a private sandy cove and the Westin Kids' Club children's play area. Disabled access.
Dragonara Rd.
Tel: (356) 21380000.
www.westinmalta.com

St Paul's Bay

Ambassador ★
Good-value hotel away from the crowds with views across St Paul's Bay.

Shipwreck Promenade, Xemxija.
Tel: (356) 21573870. www. ambassadormalta.com

Dolmen Resort Hotel ★★
High-quality seafront hotel on the Qawra Peninsula. The Oracle Casino is part of the complex. Four outdoor swimming pools and children's play area. Disabled access.
Triq Dolmen, Qawra.
Tel: (356) 23552355.
www.dolmen.com.mt

Gillieru Harbour Hotel ★★
Superb location in the harbour of St Paul's

Bay, with a popular restaurant.
Church Square.
Tel: (356) 21572720.
www.gillieru.com

San Antonio Hotel & Spa ★★
Large hotel with spa, fitness and well-being facilities and freshwater lagoon swimming pool laid out in extensive garden environment. Private beach. Disabled access.
Tourist St, Qawra.
Tel: (356) 21583434.
www.sanantonio-malta.com

Sliema

Days Inn ★
Cheap and cheerful hotel in a Sliema side street but convenient for bus routes, restaurants and the Sliema seafront. Small rooftop swimming pool. Free Wi-Fi in communal areas. 100 rooms and studio apartments.
75/76 Cathedral St.
Tel: (356) 21331162.
Email: info@iels.com.mt

Europa Hotel ★
Basic economical hotel on the Sliema seafront. Convenient for bus routes to Valletta and

A typical smaller hotel

further afield. Free car parking. Wi-Fi access and Internet café. 66 rooms and 6 self-catering studios in a building next door.

138 Tower Rd.
Tel: (356) 21334070. www. europahotel-malta.com

The Diplomat ★★

Located on the Sliema seafront. Oak-furnished air-conditioned rooms with balconies and sea views. Rooftop swimming pool. Wi-Fi access.

173 Tower Rd.
Tel: (356) 21345361 or 23497000.
www.diplomat.com.mt

Imperial ★★

Truly historic building, reflecting the Victorian age and era of British rule. The hotel has a beautiful garden, a swimming pool and separate children's pool and a games room with a snooker table. 95 rooms, including 8 adapted for guests with disabilities.

1 Rudolf St. Tel: (356) 21344093. www. imperialhotelmalta.com

Victoria Hotel ★★

Boutique hotel with an old-fashioned elegance

combined with a modern flair for comfort and hospitality. The **Copperfields Restaurant** is a superb place to wine and dine, and **The Penny Black** a great bar to stop at for a drink.

Gorg Borg Olivier St.
Tel: (356) 21334711.
www.victoriahotel.com

Fortina Spa Resort ★★★

Malta's foremost spa and luxury hotel, right beside the Tigné Point development, with splendid views across the harbour to the Valletta skyline. Some rooms are equipped with their own spa treatment facilities.

Tigné seafront.
Tel: (356) 23462346.
www.fortinasparesort.com

The Palace ★★★

Elegant boutique-style hotel, located in a quiet residential area of Sliema away from the holiday crowds but convenient for getting to all sights and attractions. There is a spa and well-being centre spread over three levels.

High St.
Tel: (356) 21333444.
www.thepalacemalta.com

Youth Hostels

Granny's Inn Hostel ★

53 Blanche Huber St.
Tel: (356) 21323762.
www.grannysinn.com

NSTS Hibernia Residence & Hostel ★

De Piro St.
Tel: (356) 25588000.
www.nsts.org

Valletta

British Hotel ★

Popular hotel with a restaurant overlooking the Grand Harbour.

40 Battery St.
Tel: (356) 21224730.
www.britishhotel.com

Grand Harbour ★

Small, good-value hotel. 24 rooms.

47 Battery St.
Tel: (356) 21246003.
www.grandharbourhotel. com

Osborne ★

Cosy, good-value hotel in Valletta's city centre.

50 South St.
Tel: (356) 21232127.
www.osbornehotel.com

Grand Hotel Excelsior ★★★

Large, modern, luxurious hotel.

Great Siege Rd, Floriana.
Tel: (356) 21250520.
www.excelsior.com.mt

Phoenicia ★★★

Elegant, luxurious
and set in mature
landscaped gardens
right beside Valletta's
City Gate and bus
station.
The Mall, Floriana.
Tel: (356) 21225241.
www.phoeniciamalta.
com

GOZO

**Maria Giovanna
Guesthouse** ★
15 rooms.
41 Rabat Rd, Marsalforn.
Tel: (356) 21553630.
www.tamariagozo.com

Calypso ★★
Pleasant hotel
overlooking Marsalforn
Bay. Rooftop terrace with
good views.
Marina St, Marsalforn.
Tel: (356) 21562000.
www.hotelcalypsogozo.
com

Cornucopia ★★
Hotel built from a
converted 18th-century
farmhouse in a Gozo
village with a selection
of bungalows.
410 Ġnien Imrik St,
Xagħra.
Tel: (356) 21556486.
www.vjborg.com/
cornucopia

San Andrea ★★
Very pleasant small
hotel overlooking
Xlendi Bay.
St Simon St, Xlendi
Promenade.
Tel: (356) 21565555.
www.hotelsanandrea.
com

**Kempinski Hotel San
Lawrenz** ★★★
First-class hotel and
spa complex set in
landscaped gardens in
the Gozo countryside.
Three restaurants,
three outdoor pools
and a separate children's
pool, and excellent spa
facilities including
Indian-style Ayurveda
massage treatments.
Triq ir-Rokon, San
Lawrenz.
Tel: (356) 22110000.
www.kempinski-gozo.com

Ta'Cenc ★★★
Well-designed single-
storey luxury
accommodation close
to cliffs overlooking
the sea. Two outdoor
pools and a spa.
Ideal base for exploring
Gozo. Disabled
access.
Sannat.
Tel: (356) 21556819.
www.vjborg.com/tacenc

Ulysses Aparthotel ★
Studios and one-bed
apartments above Moby
Dives base.
Triq il-Gostra, Xlendi.
Tel: (356) 21551616.
www.ulyssesaparthotel.
com

Baron Group ★★
40 converted farmhouses
in various locations
around Gozo.
Karlu Galea St, Victoria.
Tel: (356) 21556600.
www.barongroupmalta.
com

Gozo Farmhouses ★★
25 farmhouses converted
into luxury holiday
homes.
3 Mġarr Rd, Għajnsielem.
Tel: (356) 21561280.
www.gozofarmhouses.com

COMINO

The Comino Hotel ★★
The only
accommodation on
Comino is a four-star
hotel and bungalows,
open only for the
summer. The hotel has
its own ferry boat to
shuttle guests between
Comino, Malta and
Gozo.
Tel: (356) 21529821.
www.cominohotel.com

Practical guide

Arriving

Entry formalities

Citizens from the UK, EU countries, the USA, Canada, Australia and New Zealand may enter Malta for up to three months without a visa. Only a passport is required. South Africans need a visa.

By air

Malta International Airport

(*http://malta-airport.com*), located at Luqa, 6km (3³/₄ miles) south of Valletta, has 24-hour currency-exchange services, car-hire desks, a tourist information office, a restaurant and a variety of shops. (*For flight enquiries, tel: (356) 50043333.*)

Bus 8 links the airport with Valletta. Alternatively, there are plenty of taxis.

Air Malta, Malta's national airline, operates a scheduled service from many European destinations, including London, Manchester, Glasgow, Paris, Rome and Frankfurt. The airline also operates charter services from airports in Britain and mainland Europe.

British Airways (*www.ba.com*) operates a regular service from London Gatwick to Malta.

Ryanair flies from Luton and Dublin and **easyJet** from Belfast, Bournemouth, Gatwick, Liverpool, Newcastle and Manchester. **BMI Baby** flies from East Midlands. **Thomas Cook Airlines** has charter flights from East Midlands, Gatwick, Glasgow and Manchester.

By sea

Virtu Ferries offers a high-speed car and passenger catamaran service from Valletta Waterfront to Sicily (journey time 1 hour 30 minutes to Pozzallo and 3 hours to Catania). Schedules are published in the *Thomas Cook European Timetable.*
Ta'Xbiex Terrace, Ta'Xbiex.
Tel: (356) 23491000.
www.virtuferries.com
Also ticket sales and reservation office at Valletta Sea Passenger Terminal, Pinto Rd, Valletta. Tel: (356) 22069022. Email: res@virtuferries.com. Open: Mon–Fri 8.30am–1pm & 1.30–5pm, Sat 9am–noon.

Camping

Malta Campsite is located on Marfa Ridge and is open all year. Tents and mobile homes are available for hire. The site has a small shop, café and a swimming pool. It is some distance from public transport (about a one-hour trek) and a car can drop you to the nearest bus stop for a fee.
Tel: (356) 21521105.
www.maltacampsite.com

Camping is permitted on a piece of ground at Santa Marija Bay on Comino. There is a toilet block and the Comino Hotel bungalows and café are nearby.

Children

Parents should keep a wary eye on children if they are swimming in the sea as undercurrents are quite common. Great care should also be taken to prevent children from getting sunburnt.

An abundance of casual cafés serving pizzas, hamburgers and chips makes eating out with children an easy affair. For self-caterers, mini-markets sell familiar brands of foods, as well as baby foods and nappies.

Climate

The average temperature is over 22°C (72°F). The really hot months are from June to September when temperatures can soar to 32°C (90°F) or more. Sea breezes bring welcome relief from the heat. Less welcome is the *xlokk*, or sirocco wind, which blows from the Sahara, raising both the temperature and humidity. Autumn is warm, though storms and rain are quite frequent, particularly in October. In winter the

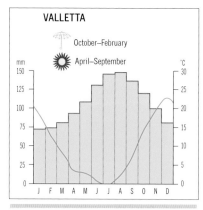

WEATHER CONVERSION CHART

25.4mm = 1 inch
°F = 1.8 × °C + 32

weather varies from warm and sunny to cold, wet and windy. Spring, which is generally considered the best time to go to Malta, is warm and sunny.

Crime

Instances of theft and serious crime are few. However, cars should not be left unlocked or valuables on display.

Customs regulations

The duty-free allowance for visitors to Malta from non-EU countries is 200 cigarettes (or the equivalent in cigars or tobacco), one litre (1¾pt) each of spirits and fortified wine, one bottle of perfume and 125g (4½oz) of eau de toilette.

Driving

Beware chaotic local drivers, potholed roads, inadequate road-signing and poor street lighting at night.

Accidents

In the event of an accident, call the police on *112* and stay with the car. For most insurance claims a police report is crucial. If you have a breakdown, call the car-hire company for aid.

Car hire

Car hire is reasonably cheap. Local law permits driving from 18 years. However, some companies will not hire cars to those aged under 25 or over 70, while others will charge extra daily insurance for doing so. Drivers must present their own national driving licence or an internationally recognised driving licence. The main international car-hire companies such as Avis and Hertz have desks at the airport and in the major resorts. Local companies are usually cheaper, but may not be quite as reliable as those of well-known companies.

Avis
50 Msida Sea Front, Msida.
Tel: (356) 25677550. www.avis.com.mt

Hertz
United House, 66 Gżira Rd, Gżira.
Tel: (356) 21333153. www.hertz.com
Also Tower Rd, Sliema, the Mellieħa Bay Hotel and at Malta International Airport Arrivals.
Tel: (356) 21314636.

Thrifty Car Rental
90 Fremond St, Qormi.
Tel: (356) 21487030. www.thrifty.com

Parking
There is a multilevel car park in Floriana with a shuttle bus service to Valletta, and the large hotels have their own car parks. However, street parking is a problem with so many cars on Malta's roads.

Petrol
Petrol or gas is sold by the litre. Service stations are open Monday–Saturday 8am–6.30pm in summer, 8am–6pm in winter. There is a rota for morning openings on Sundays and public holidays. All stations now have self-service pumps.

Regulations
Driving is on the left. The speed limit is 80kph (50mph) on highways, and 50kph

CONVERSION TABLE

FROM	TO	MULTIPLY BY
Inches	Centimetres	2.54
Feet	Metres	0.3048
Yards	Metres	0.9144
Miles	Kilometres	1.6090
Acres	Hectares	0.4047
Gallons	Litres	4.5460
Ounces	Grams	28.35
Pounds	Grams	453.6
Pounds	Kilograms	0.4536
Tons	Tonnes	1.0160

To convert back, for example from centimetres to inches, divide by the number in the third column.

(31mph) in built-up areas. The rule is that all cars approaching a roundabout must give way to the traffic already on the circuit (in theory). Seat belts must be worn, and violators can be fined. Breathalyser tests are now in force.

Electricity
240 volts, 50 cycles. Three-pin square British-style plugs are used.

Embassies and consulates
Australia *Ta'Xbiex Terrace, Ta'Xbiex.*
Tel: (356) 21338201.
Canada *103 Archbishop St, Valletta.*
Tel: (356) 25523233.
UK *Whitehall Mansions, Ta'Xbiex Sea Front, Ta'Xbiex. Tel: (356) 23230000.*
USA *Ta'Qali. Tel: (356) 25614000.*

Emergency telephone numbers
Emergency number: *112*
Ambulance: *196*
Fire: *199*
Police: *191*

Health

Malta has very good modern health services and healthcare is free to EU citizens on production of a European Health Insurance Card or EHIC (*www.ehic.org.uk*). This covers emergency hospital treatment but not medicine bought from a pharmacy, and is not a substitute for travel insurance.

There are government health centres in all towns and larger villages. The main hospital on Malta is **Mater Dei**, Birkirkara (*tel: (356) 25450000*); on Gozo it is the **Gozo General Hospital** in Victoria (*tel: (356) 21561600*). Both accept the EHIC. Numerous private hospitals on the islands offer treatment for a fee.

If you need a doctor urgently, your hotel reception will have a number to call. Many local pharmacies have a doctor available for consultation. If you are taking regular medication and need fresh supplies while staying in Malta, it is advisable to take a prescription or doctor's letter with you.

Visitors from Australia, the USA, Canada and Europe do not require certificates of vaccination or inoculation to enter Malta.

LANGUAGE

English is spoken almost everywhere, and it is not necessary to know any Maltese (Malti). It does help, however, if you can master basic pronunciation, particularly for place names, which do not sound at all how you might expect. The following is a basic and approximate guide to the pronunciation of those letters that cause the most confusion, using the nearest English equivalent.

For those who feel tempted to give Maltese a go, here are a few basic phrases.

yes	iva
no	le
please	jekk jogħġbok
thank you	grazzi
good morning	bonġu
good evening	bonswa
goodbye	saħħa
How are you?	Kif int?
excuse me	skużi
How much?	Kemm?
What is your name?	X'ismek?
My name is . . .	Jisimni . . .
Where is . . .?	Fejn hu . . .?
right	lemin
left	xellug
One	Wieħed
Five	Hamsa
Ten	Ghaxra
Twenty	Ghoxrin
Fifty	Hamsin
One hundred	Mija
One thousand	Elf

MALTESE–ENGLISH PRONUNCIATION

ċ - ch ġ - j

għ - silent

h - silent, except at the end of a word when it is aspirated

ħ - h j - y

m - m, except if the initial M is followed by a consonant, when it becomes im. (Mdina is therefore 'imDEEna'.)

q - silent x - sh

ż - tz z - z

Tap water is safe to drink, but is heavily chlorinated and may taste strange. Bottled water is readily available in grocery shops and supermarkets.

Insurance

Personal travel insurance, available from Thomas Cook travel agents, tour operators or insurance companies, should give adequate cover for medical expenses, loss or theft, personal liability (but liability arising from motor accidents is not usually included) and cancellation expenses. Carefully check that the amount of cover is adequate.

If you hire a car, collision insurance, often called collision damage waiver or CDW, is normally offered by the hirer, and is usually compulsory. Check, before you leave home, whether your own car insurance policy covers you. If not, CDW must be paid locally: this can be as much as 50 per cent of the hiring fee.

Neither CDW nor your personal travel insurance will protect you for liability arising out of an accident in a hired car if, for example, you damage another vehicle or injure someone. If you are likely to hire a car, obtain such cover before you go.

Media

The English-language papers are *The Times* (daily), which leans slightly to the right of centre, the *Sunday Times* and the *Malta Independent* (daily and Sundays). In Valletta and Sliema major foreign newspapers are usually available in the late afternoon of the day of publication. On Gozo, foreign newspapers arrive the following day.

Radio Malta broadcasts in both Maltese and English. The BBC World Service can be picked up on short wave. Most hotels carry the Sky News channel on TVs in guest rooms.

Money matters

Banks are normally open until early afternoon from Monday to Friday and until midday on Saturday. Some branches in tourist areas work longer hours. Summer and winter opening hours may differ.

Malta's currency is the euro (€). Major credit cards, traveller's cheques and Eurocheques, backed by a guarantee card, are all widely accepted. ATMs can be found at the airport and in all towns and main villages. Many shops accept British pounds and US dollars. No commission is charged for changing foreign cash.

The two major banks, HSBC and the Bank of Valletta, have branches all over the island, open Monday to Friday 8.30am–2pm (some also open on Friday afternoon), and on Saturday at 8–11.30am or 8.30am–noon. Foreign exchange facilities at banks normally stay open for the afternoon. There are 24-hour bank exchange facilities at Malta International Airport, and 24-hour automatic foreign exchange machines in Valletta and main resorts. Hotels may exchange foreign currency but at less favourable rates than banks.

If you need to transfer money quickly, you can use the MoneyGram℠ Money Transfer service (*www.moneygram.com*). (*For more details in the UK, telephone Freephone 0800 897198.*)

National holidays

On these dates, offices, museums, monuments and most shops will be closed.

1 January New Year's Day
10 February Feast of St Paul's Shipwreck
19 March Feast of St Joseph
31 March Freedom Day
Variable Good Friday
1 May Workers' Day
7 June *Sette giugno* (Commemoration of 7 June 1919)
29 June Feast of St Peter and St Paul
15 August Feast of the Assumption
8 September Victory Day
21 September Independence Day
8 December Feast of the Immaculate Conception
13 December Republic Day
25 December Christmas Day

Opening hours
Museums

The majority of the museums on the islands are government-run and have standard hours: daily 9am–5pm, last admission 4.30pm. Entrance fees vary, depending on the site or museum.

Shops

Shops are normally open 9am–1pm and 4–7pm. In tourist areas many shops remain open to 10pm. Most shops are closed on Sundays and public holidays.

Organised tours

Several companies offer a selection of fully guided tours of the islands. Prices compare favourably with excursions in other parts of Europe. If you want to explore Valletta and Mdina, you will probably get more enjoyment by going independently and browsing at your leisure. For those without a car, the full-day island tours are a good way of seeing the highlights. When making a reservation, check if the price includes the boat trip to the Blue Grotto: some companies don't warn you of this extra cost. The numerous boat excursions include trips around the islands and the Valletta harbour cruise (*see pp48–9*). One- and two-day excursions are offered to Sicily.

Pharmacies

Pharmacists are well qualified and pharmacies (or chemists) are stocked with most well-known medicines. They keep normal shop opening times from Monday to Saturday. On Sundays they open on a rota, one in each district and for the morning only. Consult the English-language newspapers for details.

Places of worship

The Maltese are devoutly Catholic, but all religions are tolerated. Mass is generally celebrated in Maltese, but in

Valletta, Sliema, St Julian's, Rabat, St Paul's Bay and Mellieħa there are services in English on Sunday mornings.

Church of England services are held in Valletta at St Paul's Anglican Cathedral and the Bible Baptist Church, and, in Sliema, at the Holy Trinity Church.

Police

The police headquarters is in Floriana (*tel: (356) 21224001–9*). The police wear a dark blue uniform in winter, light blue in summer. The number for police on Gozo is *(356) 21562040*. Every village has a police station, open 24 hours.

Post office

The Maltese postal service, operated by Malta Post, is cheap and efficient. Stamps are sold at post offices, most hotels with newsagents, and in many shops. The **Main Post Office** is at 305 Qormi Road, Qormi. The opening hours are Monday to Friday 8am–1pm and 1.30–3.30pm. Other post offices are open Monday to Saturday 7.30am– 12.45pm. The main **Gozo Post Office** is at 129 Republic Street, Victoria.

Public transport
Buses

The quaint old British Bedford and Leyland buses are being replaced by more environmentally friendly modern buses. The bus service on Malta is an extremely cheap way of getting around, but you cannot rely on it if you are in a hurry. Buses don't run to timetables and are unreliable in the evenings.

Most bus routes radiate from the Valletta terminus and a few from the Sliema Waterfront. There is very little route information at bus stops or in stations. Finding your bus in Valletta's bus station can be quite a trial; take care crossing from one stand to another among the moving buses.

You buy single-trip tickets from the bus driver as you board; always carry some small change for bus fares. The price of a ticket varies according to the number of zones you pass through; if you use the bus a lot, buying an all-zone pass for unlimited travel for one, three, five or seven days is a good idea. Information about Malta's bus services is available from the Public Transport Association (*tel: (356) 21250007; www.atp.com.mt*).

On Gozo, you can generally depend on route 25, which links Mġarr ferry terminal to Victoria (and in summer Marsalforn and Xlendi) and is timed to meet the ferries.

Malta Sightseeing is a hop-on, hop-off service on open-top double-decker buses with a boat tour included. They run between 9am and 5.30pm.

Electric cabs

City Cabs operate small electric taxis the size of golf-course buggies, and will take you anywhere within Valletta but not outside the walls. *Tel: (056) 21333321.*

Ferries

The **Gozo Channel Company** (*tel: (356) 22109000; www.gozochannel.com*)

operates a car and passenger ferry service between Ċirkewwa at the northern tip of Malta and Mġarr Harbour on Gozo. In summer boats go every 45 minutes in the daytime and on busy days a shuttle service operates. Less frequent crossings are made from midnight to 6am. The journey takes 25 minutes.

The ferry service is sometimes suspended if the sea is rough – it is wise to phone ahead to check. If you are crossing with a car, you should arrive in good time; there are no advance reservations and long queues soon build up. Passengers with reduced mobility can get assistance by phoning at least an hour before departure.

The Gozo Channel Company also operates a cargo service with passengers from Sa Maison pier at Pieta Creek near Valletta. The journey time is 90 minutes and runs once a day on Monday, Tuesday and Thursday.

The Marsamxetto Ferry is the fastest way of crossing the harbour between Valletta and Sliema during the daytime. It takes about five minutes and runs every half an hour until 6pm.

The *Thomas Cook European Timetable* has full details of ferry times. Get a copy from Thomas Cook branches in the UK or by phoning *01733 416477.*

Helicopters

You can make the journey between Malta International Airport and Gozo very rapidly by helicopter transfer. Helicopter tours of Malta are great for photography and sightseeing. *Heli Tours Malta. Tel: (056) 23696442. www.heli-link-malta.com*

Karrozzins

The *karrozzin* is an old-fashioned horse-drawn cab which will take you through the streets of Valletta, Sliema or Mdina. They wait at various tourist locations around Valletta. You should negotiate a price as they are usually expensive, but they have the great benefit of a shady ride instead of a long walk in the baking sun.

Motorbikes and bicycles

Several companies have motorbikes, quad bikes and bicycles for hire around the islands. Main roads have been improved with EU funding but country roads remain potholed and rough. Take care as the traffic is fast and unpredictable, though less so on Gozo.

Aquarius *188 St Paul's St, St Paul's Bay. Tel: (356) 21575736.*
On Two Wheels *36 Rabat Rd, Marsalforn. Tel: (356) 21561503.*

Seaplanes

Harbour Air (*tel: (356) 21228302; www.harbourairmalta.com*) operates a daily scheduled seaplane service between the Sea Passenger Terminal on the Valletta Waterfront and Mġarr Marina on Gozo. The journey time is about 15 minutes and you get a splendid view of Malta on the way.

Taxis

Taxis are readily available at the airport, in Valletta at City Gate and Palace Square, on the Strand in Sliema and at other main tourist centres. A fixed-fare booking service operates at the airport, but elsewhere, the cost of a taxi ride is a perennial bone of contention as drivers rarely use their meters; make sure you agree a fare beforehand. If you feel you have been overcharged by a taxi driver, you should report the matter with the driver's identity number to the tourist office.

A more reliable and economical way of arranging transport is to book a private hire car in advance for an agreed price.

Marshall Group

Chauffeur-driven private hire cars.
Tel: (356) 21691007.
www.marshallgroup.com.mt

Wembley's Cars

24-hour taxi service and private hire based in Paceville.
Tel: (356) 21374141.
www.wembleys.net

Zarb Coaches

Private hire vehicles including a minibus adapted for wheelchairs.
Tel: (356) 21489991.
www.zarbcoaches.com

You may find that hiring a self-drive car is the most economical option. Local car rental is cheap and the airlines have good deals with big-name rental companies such as Avis, Budget and Hertz.

Water taxis

The best way to travel between Valletta and the Vittoriosa Waterfront is by crossing the Grand Harbour in a *dgħajsa* (pronounced 'dicer'), a colourful former fishing boat now operating as a water taxi. They can be hired for a private tour.

A & S Water Taxis *19 Triq Kappillan Frangisk Azzopardi, Senglea.*
Tel: (356) 21806921.
www.maltesewatertaxis.com

Dgħajsa Cooperative
Tel: (056) 79620034.

Senior citizens

Entrance to state museums is half price to over-65s. Unlike in other EU countries, car-hire companies have no upper age limit, but some are reluctant to hire to over-70s. Malta attracts a lot of older visitors. The following tour operators specialise in holidays for them:

Saga Holidays Ltd
Saga Building, Middelburg Square, Folkestone, Kent, CT20 1AZ, UK.
Tel: (01303) 771111.

Saga International Holidays
222 Berkley Street, Boston, Massachusetts 02116, USA. Tel: (617) 262 2262.

Smoking

Smoking is banned in public places apart from separate, designated areas.

Sustainable tourism

Thomas Cook is a strong advocate of ethical and fairly traded tourism and believes that the travel experience should be as good for the places visited as it is for the people who visit them. That's why we firmly support The Travel Foundation, a charity that develops solutions to help improve and protect holiday destinations, their environment, traditions and culture. To find out what you can do to make a positive difference to the places you travel to and the people who live there, please visit *www.makeholidaysgreener.org.uk*

Telephones and Internet
The British-style red telephone boxes are poorly maintained and only take phonecards when they do work.

Malta uses the GSM900 mobile phone network, which is compatible with the rest of Europe, Australia and New Zealand. Roaming charges for mobile phones in Malta are the same as elsewhere in Europe and you will be charged for receiving calls. If you plan on using your mobile frequently, you can buy a local SIM card from branches of mobile phone operators Go, Vodaphone Malta and Melita Mobile.

Internet cafés are established in most tourist areas. Leisure complexes and shopping malls have Internet zones. Most hotels have at least one computer available for guests to go online, and good ones offer free Wi-Fi access in the room.

Useful international telephone codes:
Australia *00 61*
Ireland *00 353*

New Zealand *00 64*
UK *00 44*
USA and Canada *00 1*
Overseas Operator *1152*
Local Enquiries *1182*

Time
Malta time is one hour ahead of Greenwich Mean Time (GMT) in winter, and two hours ahead in summer (from late March until late September).

Tipping
If the service charge in a restaurant is not included, it is normal to leave 10 per cent. Taxi drivers don't necessarily expect to be tipped. Car-park attendants at free car parks will expect a tip.

Tourist guides
Few people know Malta and Gozo better than the professional tourist guides – you will find that they have the knowledge and experience to make your visit memorable. They will know the quickest ways of getting from one place to another and where the best places are to eat or have fun. The VisitMalta website has a list of licensed guides (*see www.visitmalta.com for further information*).

Tourist offices
Malta Tourism Authority's HQ and tourist enquiry office: *Auberge d'Italie, Merchants' St, Valletta.*
Tel: (356) 22915440. Fax: (356) 22915893.

Malta tourist information offices:
*Malta International Airport
(tel: (356) 23696073); Tigrija Palazz
shopping centre, Republic St, Victoria,
Gozo (tel: (356) 21561419); Torre dello
Standardo, Mdina.*
Gozo Tourism Association: *5 George
Borg Olivier St Victoria, Gozo.
Tel: (356) 21565171.
www.islandofgozo.org*
Malta Tourism Authority in London:
*Unit C, Park House, 14 Northfields,
London SW18 1DD.
Tel: (020) 8874 9416.*

Websites
www.visitmalta.com
Malta Tourism Authority's
comprehensive website.
www.aboutmalta.com
Lively online guide to everything
about Malta.
www.starwebmalta.com
Informative and comprehensive
directory and reviews of
accommodation, restaurants, bars,
recreational services and shopping.
www.atp.com.mt
The Passenger Transport Association's
guide to bus services in Malta.
www.restaurantsmalta.com
Online version of the *Definitive(ly)
Good Guide to Restaurants in Malta
and Gozo.*

Travellers with disabilities
Valletta, Mdina and Victoria on Gozo
are particularly difficult places to
negotiate for travellers in wheelchairs.

Many hotels, some museums and a few
prehistoric sites have introduced ramps
and toilet adaptations. The new Visitor
Centre at Ħaġar Qim, for example, has
been designed with full disabled access
in mind, but the Hypogeum complex in
Paola is accessible only by stairs beyond
the lobby exhibition.

For information about disabled
access, contact the **National
Commission for the Disabled** (*Centro
Hidma Socjali, Triq Braille, Santa
Venera; tel: (356) 2148 7789;
www.knpd.org*).

The hotel section of the Malta
Tourism Authority's VisitMalta website
indicates which ones have facilities
suitable for visitors with disabilities.

Index

Acknowledgements

Thomas Cook wishes to thank the photographers, picture libraries and other organisations for the loan of the photographs reproduced in this book, to whom copyright in the photographs belongs.

ALAMY 95 (IAIN DAINTY), 96 (PRISMA/KREDER KATJA), 137 (PRISMA/KREDER KATJA), 169 (SIMON READY); DAVID BROWNE 143; DREAMSTIME 1 (RAINER SCHMITTCHEN), 73 (STANISLAV SOKOLOV), 76 (SASOYKC), 91 (MORRISON), 92 (OLEG SHIPOV), 130 (MCCARTHYSTUDIO), 137 (JACEK MALIPAN), 140 (FEDERICO CHINI), 141 (REUBEN DEMANUELE), 171 (SVETLNA TIKHONOVA); DREAMSTIME/RVS 49; FLICKR/H-ANGELE 28, FLICKR/GLEN BOWMAN 94, FLICKR/PAPALARS 159; FOTOLIA/RENÉ AIGNER 147, FOTOLIA/WILLIAM ATTARD MCCARTHY 162; courtesy of MALTA TOURISM AUTHORITY (www.visitmalta.com) 14, 16, 25, 27b, 29a, 40, 41, 43, 58, 67, 75, 87, 113, 118, 132, 138, 139, 149; MARY EVANS PICTURE LIBRARY 17; MATTHEW MIRABELLI 10, 13, 19, 21, 22, 23, 27a, 31, 44, 69, 81, 83, 90, 102, 121, 145, 146, 148, 153, 154, 157; THOMAS COOK 35, 60, 86, 117, 151, 155; W VOYSEY 7, 11, 15, 45, 66, 68, 74, 78, 79, 93, 98, 114, 123, 136, 168; WIKIMEDIA COMMONS/H J MOYES 63 The remaining pictures are held in the AA PHOTO LIBRARY and were taken by PHILIP ENTICKNAP

For CAMBRIDGE PUBLISHING MANAGEMENT LTD:
Project editor: Ed Robinson
Typesetter: Donna Pedley
Proofreaders: Karolin Thomas & Kelly Walker
Indexer: Marie Lorimer

SEND YOUR THOUGHTS TO
BOOKS@THOMASCOOK.COM

We're committed to providing the very best up-to-date information in our travel guides and constantly strive to make them as useful as they can be. You can help us to improve future editions by letting us have your feedback. If you've made a wonderful discovery on your travels that we don't already feature, if you'd like to inform us about recent changes to anything that we do include, or if you simply want to let us know your thoughts about this guidebook and how we can make it even better – we'd love to hear from you.

Send us ideas, discoveries and recommendations today and then look out for your valuable input in the next edition of this title.

Emails to the above address, or letters to the traveller guides Series Editor, Thomas Cook Publishing, PO Box 227, Coningsby Road, Peterborough PE3 8SB, UK.

Please don't forget to let us know which title your feedback refers to!